Unleashing
HEAVEN'S
Blessings

D0981372

HAPPY
Caldwell

WHITAKER
HOUSE

UNLEASHING HEAVEN'S BLESSINGS

Power to Overcome Limitations in Your Life
Revised and updated edition
(Based on the previously published title *No More Limits!*)

Pastor Happy Caldwell
Agape Church, Inc.
P.O. Box 22007
Little Rock, AR 72221-2007
501-225-0612
www.agape-church.org

ISBN: 978-1-60374-276-4
Printed in the United States of America
© 1999, 2011 by Howard Caldwell

Whitaker House
1030 Hunt Valley Circle
New Kensington, PA 15068
www.whitakerhouse.com

Library of Congress Cataloging-in-Publication Data

Caldwell, Happy.
  Unleashing heaven's blessings / Happy Caldwell. — Rev. and updated.
    p. cm.
  Rev. ed. of: No more limits.
  Summary: "Explains how Christians can overcome spiritual, financial, emotional, and physical limitations through faith and God's power, which enables them to move past their boundaries and enter into the fullness of the life God has planned for them"—Provided by publisher.
  ISBN 978-1-60374-276-4 (trade pbk. : alk. paper) 1. Success—Religious aspects—Christianity. I. Caldwell, Happy. No more limits. II. Title.
  BV4598.3.C32 2011
  248.4—dc22
                    2011015484

1 2 3 4 5 6 7 8 9 10   **W**   17 16 15 14 13 12 11

DEDICATION

"Now to Him who is able to do exceedingly abundantly above all that we ask or think, according to the power that works in us, to Him be glory in the church by Christ Jesus to all generations, forever and ever. Amen."

—Ephesians 3:20–21

Contents

Exceeding the "Impossible"

Prior to May 1954, most of the sports world thought that it was impossible to run a mile in under four minutes. Runners had failed for decades to break the four-minute-mile barrier. It was seen as an obstacle, both physical and psychological, that exceeded human limits.

However, on May 6, 1954, a medical student at Oxford University named Roger Bannister broke the four-minute-mile barrier, proving that seemingly impossible limits can be broken.

Recognize Your Biggest Obstacle

The first thing that Bannister did to achieve this feat was wonder whether the biggest obstacle runners faced might not be their own beliefs or fears. After all, with better running conditions and better training, someone could possibly run a mile in less than four minutes.

He became fascinated by the challenge of proving that this limit was self-imposed. In his book, *The Four-Minute Mile*, he wrote, "The four-minute mile had become rather like an Everest....It was a barrier that seemed to defy all attempts to break it."[1]

Sound familiar? What about the limits in your life—do they scream back at you and defy your attempts to push them out of your way? Could your biggest obstacle be your thoughts and fears about those limits?

RENEW YOUR MIND WITH THE WORD OF GOD

Bannister studied the problem as you would any scientific experiment. That increased his understanding of the common sense approach to its resolution. He read up on the physiology of breaking the barrier and confirmed in himself that it was possible.

Similarly, when we renew our minds with the Word of God and hear what the Word says, then faith comes. When faith comes, fear goes. When fear knocks on the door, faith answers it, but there is no one there, because faith has driven it away. When we identify our limits, we can confront them and overcome them by acting on God's Word.

A father once implored Jesus to deliver his son from demon possession, which was causing the boy terrible seizures.

> [The man said,] *"If You can do anything, have compassion on us and help us." Jesus said to him, "If you can believe, all things are possible to him who believes." Immediately the father of the child cried out and said with tears, "Lord, I believe; help my unbelief!"* (Mark 9:22–24)

---

1. Roger Bannister, *The Four-Minute Mile* (New York: Lyons & Burford, Publishers, 1981), 188–189.

Unbelief sets limits. When we realize it is our own unbelief that has set many of the limitations in our lives, we can remove those limitations with our faith.

BUILD SPIRITUAL STRENGTH AND ENDURANCE

Roger Bannister began building strength and endurance to break the four-minute-mile barrier that had challenged runners for years.

He trained to exhaustion in thirty-minute workouts and cross-trained to build stamina. He ran uphill and downhill on grass to strengthen the muscles in the backs of his legs. One month before the race, he went hiking to clear his head and focus his concentration. Five days before the race, he rested.

The day of the race, the weather was less than perfect. In fact, Bannister considered not running, but he realized, "I had reached my peak physically and psychologically. There would never be another day like it."[2] Still, high winds almost caused him to postpone trying for the record. Then, he said,

> As we lined up for the start I glanced at the flag again. It fluttered more gently now, and the scene from Shaw's *Saint Joan* flashed through my mind, how she, at her desperate moment, waited for the wind to change. Yes, the wind was dropping slightly. This was the moment when I made my decision. The attempt was on.[3]

During the race, Bannister refused to give in to crushing fatigue, as well as to oxygen debt. "My body had

---

2. Bannister, *Four-Minute Mile*, 209.

3. Bannister, *Four-Minute Mile*, 212.

long since exhausted all its energy, but it went on running just the same," he said.[4]

As Bannister lunged forward into the finish line tape, he fell exhausted into supporting arms and awaited confirmation that he had broken the limit. He had run the mile in 3:59:04!

Building spiritual strength and endurance will also help you to break your barriers and set precedents of victory in your life. *"Let us lay aside every weight, and the sin which so easily ensnares us, and let us run with endurance the race that is set before us"* (Hebrews 12:1).

OVERCOME YOUR LIMITATIONS!

By the end of 1955, four other runners had broken the limit of the four-minute mile. In this book, you will learn that there are no more limitations for the child of God, and that faith and spiritual power will unleash heaven's blessings in your life. Just as Roger Bannister broke a limit in the natural realm, we are called by God to break limits in the spiritual realm. When we do so, we will inspire others to do the same. God is saying to us, "No more limits!"

---

4. Ibid., 214.

CHAPTER ONE

YOU ARE AN OVERCOMER

Millions of people are wearing shoes, shirts, and hats with a biblical message imprinted on them, and they don't even know it. I am talking about people who have bought shoes and clothes displaying the Nike, Inc., logo.

BE A "NIKE" PERSON

Nike is actually a biblical word. It is the Greek word translated as "*victory*" in 1 John 5:4 and is pronounced nee-kay. This word also means "conquest" and "success."

> *For whatever is born of God overcomes the world. And this is the victory [nike] that has overcome the world; our faith.*   (1 John 5:4)

When I first discovered that *nike* meant victory, conquest, and success, I became excited and went out and bought myself three hats, a pair of tennis shoes, and two shirts with the Nike logo on them, as a personal reminder that I could overcome and be victorious through faith in Christ. I am not endorsing Nike, Inc., or its sporting apparel, but I want to emphasize for you what the word *nike* means.

You can explain to other people that *nike* is in the Bible, and that the real "Nike Man" is Jesus Christ. Jesus died so that we can be victorious in this life and the life to come. Tell others that they, too, can be "*nike* people" in Jesus.

LEAVE THE DEVIL IN THE DUST

The Nike logo looks like a checkmark and is called a "swoosh." The meaning of the swoosh is basically "Leave them in the dust."

Spiritually, whom should we be leaving in the dust? It isn't other people, but rather our enemy, Satan, or the devil, who "wrestles" against us and throws obstacles in our paths to defeat us. (See Ephesians 6:12.)

In the Bible, the devil is generally represented or symbolized by a serpent. In the garden of Eden, after the serpent succeeded in tempting human beings to disobey God, God cursed him in this way:

> *Because you have done this, you are cursed more than all cattle, and more than every beast of the field; on your belly you shall go, and you shall eat dust all the days of your life.* (Genesis 3:14)

The serpent was used by the devil, and God told the serpent it was going to eat dust. Did you know that the devil has been "swooshed" by God?

First John 5:4 says, *"Whatever is born of God overcomes the world."* Jesus overcame the world. He overcame death, hell, and everything else, including the devil, who is also called *"the god of this world"* (2 Corinthians 4:4 KJV) and *"the prince of the power of the air"* (Ephesians 2:2). Jesus has overcome all!

When you accept Jesus Christ as your Lord and Savior, you are an overcomer, because you are now part of God's family. You are *"born again"* (John 3:3), which is the same as being *"born of God."* It means you have a share in the spoils of Jesus' victory over the devil. This is not because of anything you have done. In yourself, you could not overcome the devil, but, through Jesus, you share in His victory.

Therefore, *nike* people are victors over the devil through Jesus. *Nike* people leave the devil in the dust.

AN IMAGE OF SUCCESS AND VICTORY

Nike, Inc., used to have the advertising slogan "Just Do It!" The corporation has been very successful in marketing its products to consumers over the years. As I indicated earlier, Nike is not just selling sporting apparel, but it is also selling an image of success and victory. Nike wants you to feel like you are a winner when you buy its clothing and equipment, and it does this by associating its products with winners in the sports world.

A major reason for the company's success is that personal image is very important in our society. People wear all kinds of things to project a successful image. They dress in designer clothing to make a statement. They want to indicate they have arrived by wearing a certain garment or a particular brand of shoes. And people are willing to pay a lot to wear the "right" clothes and shoes; a pair of fancy tennis shoes is expensive.

So, when people wear the Nike brand, they are identifying with a logo and an image that signifies, "I am a victor. I am a conqueror. I have arrived."

IDENTIFY WITH JESUS

Sadly, our society takes its understanding of what it means to be a winner more from the subtle message of a Nike logo on a tennis shoe than it does from the word *Christian*. Yet, those who are Christians are born of God and, through Jesus, are true victors. Through Jesus, we are overcomers and have success.

It is good for you to identify with being a conqueror and a winner. God wants you to identify with Jesus Christ: Jesus is a victor. Jesus is a conqueror. Jesus is a success.

The garments you wear on the outside are not really important. The important thing is to understand who you are in Christ. Say, "In Jesus, I am a winner! In Jesus, I am an overcomer! In Jesus, I am a conqueror! In Jesus, I have arrived!"

God wants you to see a new spiritual image of yourself by identifying with the victories of Jesus. Remember that Jesus overcame hell, death, and the grave. He defeated all the enemies we will ever encounter. There is no greater name than the name of Jesus. You are entitled to partake of the benefits belonging to Jesus Christ, and you share in His inheritance. Grasp these truths in your mind, and you will remove all the limitations that are keeping you from doing what God wants you to do.

> GOD WANTS YOU TO SEE A NEW SPIRITUAL IMAGE OF YOURSELF BY IDENTIFYING WITH THE VICTORIES OF JESUS.

The Word of God says you are triumphant in Jesus (see 2 Corinthians 2:14), so line up your thinking with the Word. This is not about the power of positive thinking. It is much more than that. It is about the power of the positive Word of God. When you have God's Word in you, and it begins to renew your mind, it will change you into the person God desires you to be. God's Word in you will make you a victorious overcomer through all the challenges of life.

There are no limits to what you can do through Jesus. Rejoice in the fact that you are born of God. Again, the Bible says, *"For whatever is born of God overcomes the world. And this is the victory that has overcome the world; our faith"* (1 John 5:4).

GOD HAS A PLAN FOR YOUR SUCCESS AND VICTORY

YOU HAVE A DIVINE DESTINY

God told the Old Testament prophet Jeremiah that He knew him before he was born.

> *Before I formed you in the womb I knew*
> *you; before you were born I sanctified you; I*
> *ordained you a prophet to the nations.*
> (Jeremiah 1:5)

The book of Romans says that God also knew *you* before you were born. Think about this fact for a moment. Your existence is no accident. God knew you from eternity, and He watched over you as you were being formed in your mother's womb. He had a plan for your life. He foreknew you and predestined you to be conformed to the image of His Son Jesus.

> *For whom He foreknew, He also predes-*
> *tined to be conformed to the image of His*
> *Son, that He might be the firstborn among*
> *many brethren.* (Romans 8:29)

God prepared the way for you to be born again, or saved, and to take on Jesus' very nature. However, it is up to you whether you will take advantage of what He has prepared for you. God knows all things, and He has a wonderful purpose for your life, but He gives you a free will. He has given you the right to decide whether to be born again, and He has given you the right to choose to seek Him and receive all that He has planned for you.

You can seek God and find out His will for your life. Jesus made this possible by His sacrificial death on the cross on your behalf, and by His resurrection. Now, it is up to you to make good choices and to follow Him daily.

YOU ARE CALLED, JUSTIFIED, AND GLORIFIED

Moreover whom He predestined, these He also called; whom He called, these He also justified; and whom He justified, these He also glorified. (Romans 8:30)

God has called you. If you have responded to that call through faith in Christ Jesus, He has justified you. When God justified you, He took away all charges of wrongdoing against you. He removed your sins and gave you new life in Christ. You now have the right to go before Him with a pure heart. He gave you this new life so that you can fulfill His plan for you.

God has glorified you through His grace, and He wants you to take your place with Jesus in heaven. You do not deserve to be glorified. Your glory is a reflection of the glory of God within you. This glory is part of the new nature you received when you accepted Jesus Christ as your Savior and were born again.

It is essential for you to realize that God truly has a plan for your life, and that He has called you, justified you, and glorified you through His Son Jesus. Spiritually, legally, God has caused you to sit with Him in heavenly places. He has given you all the necessary ingredients to be successful in this life and forever. This is His gift to you.

Even when we were dead in trespasses, [God] made us alive together with Christ (by grace you have been saved), and raised us up together, and made us sit together in the heavenly places in Christ Jesus, that in the ages to come He might show the exceeding riches of His grace in His kindness toward us in Christ Jesus. For by grace you have been saved through faith, and that not of yourselves; it is the gift of God.

(Ephesians 2:5–8)

IF GOD IS FOR YOU, WHO CAN BE AGAINST YOU?

Your position in Christ in the heavenly places also carries with it some rights here on earth. God is working on your behalf. He is able to keep you from failing. He wants you to fulfill His plan for your life. Those who oppose God cannot prevail against the plans He has for you.

> GOD IS WORKING ON YOUR BEHALF. HE WANTS YOU TO FULFILL HIS PLAN FOR YOUR LIFE.

In Romans 8:31, the apostle Paul asked a good follow-up question to his previous statement, "*Moreover whom He predestined, these He also called; whom He called, these He also justified; and whom He justified, these He also glorified*" (verse 30). His question was,

What then shall we say to these things?

Think about this question and give your own reply. How will you respond? What will you say about the fact that God has called, justified, and glorified you through His Son Jesus?

Paul then gave us the answer to *"What then shall we say to these things?"* (This is an open-book test.) He wrote,

> *If God is for us, who can be against us?*
> (Romans 8:31)

This is a wonderful promise that applies to you. God is on your side! He is for you and not against you.

Personalize this promise and say it out loud: "If God is for me, who can be against me?" God's plan for your life includes the security that nobody and nothing can prevail against you when you are fulfilling His divine purpose and destiny for your life.

You Have Freely Been Given All Things

Yes, God is on your side. He is not holding back His blessings.

> *He who did not spare His own Son, but delivered Him up for us all, how shall He not with Him also freely give us all things?*
> (Romans 8:32)

This verse says that God has freely given us *"all things."* *"All things"* is not restrictive. *"All things"* means that there are no limits to what God has freely given you. His plan is to give you all things.

You Are a Superchampion Through the Love of Jesus

Since God has freely given you all things, nothing can happen to you that will keep His love from you. He has destined you to be more than a conqueror over the circumstances of life.

> *Yet in all these things we are more than conquerors through Him who loved us.*
> (Romans 8:37)

The Greek word translated as the phrase "*more than conquerors*" is *hupernikao*. The first part of this word is the prefix *huper*. The modern equivalent of this word in English is "hyper." Hyper means "above," "beyond," "super," "more than," or "excessive." The verb *nikao* comes from the root word that we have just been looking at: *nike*, or "victory." *Nikao* therefore means "to subdue," "to conquer," "to prevail," or "to overcome." Put the two words together, and *hupernikao* means "to vanquish beyond," "to more than conquer," or "to overwhelmingly conquer." In other words, the Bible tells us that we are superovercomers, or supervictors!

When you are born again, you can claim the title of supervictor through Jesus. You are not a supervictor in yourself but in Him. He has *already* won the victory. You are taking your place alongside Him.

> **YOU HAVE THE ABILITY TO DO WHATEVER GOD HAS CALLED YOU TO DO.**

You are more than a conqueror because Jesus won the victory. You can therefore personalize Romans 8:37 and proclaim, "I am more than a conqueror through Him who loved me."

This fact is the reason you have the ability to do whatever God has called you to do. God reveals Himself to us as we study

His Word. As you read your Bible prayerfully, you will begin to understand how much God really wants to bless you and cause you to be victorious in life. And, when you have the Word of God in your heart (see Psalm 119:11), it will renew your mind, and it will change you. When your mind is renewed, you will become convinced that these things are true. When this happens, your life will never be the same.

NOTHING CAN KEEP GOD'S LOVE FROM YOU

The apostle Paul was convinced that the love of God was stronger than any opposing circumstances he faced in life.

> *For I am persuaded that neither death nor life, nor angels nor principalities nor powers, nor things present nor things to come, nor height nor depth, nor any other created thing, shall be able to separate us from the love of God which is in Christ Jesus our Lord.* (Romans 8:38–39)

To be persuaded means to be strongly convinced. It means you have settled the issue in your mind, and your belief is unshakable. Paul was persuaded that there were no circumstances—not even death itself—that could separate him from the love of God in Christ Jesus.

You, also, should be persuaded that you are more than a conqueror over death and all adverse circumstances. Jesus conquered everything, and you have nothing to fear. Angels, principalities, powers, things present, things to come, height, depth— nothing can separate you from the love of God.

Since Jesus has overcome all—everything in the world, the devil, death, and hell—there is nothing to fear. Be persuaded that, through Jesus, you are an overcomer. You have been made more than a conqueror through Jesus, who loved you and died for you.

There Is No Limit to What You Can Accomplish

You Can Do It

There are no limits, therefore, to what you can accomplish as God works through you and in your life. Paul knew the power of God was working in him when he said, *"I can do all things through Christ who strengthens me"* (Philippians 4:13).

Paul was convinced that Christ was his strength, and that he could do all things. This statement applies to you, too. Personalize it for yourself.

When Jesus lives in you, He will strengthen you. In your own strength, you can do nothing, but in the strength of God, you can do all things. God has given you everything you need to be successful in accomplishing His purposes for your life. Even though you may be weak, there is no limit to what you can do through Jesus Christ. There is nothing to prevent you from being victorious. Jesus has made it all possible for you! His victory is your victory. His life is your life. His peace and joy are your peace and joy. God has freely given you everything in Christ Jesus that you need to be an overcomer.

Push Your Limits

Since there are no hindrances to fulfilling God's purpose and plan for your life, push your limits out as far as they will go. "Pushing your limits" does not mean you should do something crazy. God does things *"decently and in order"* (1 Corinthians 14:40). Rather, pushing your limits means...

- you recognize God has a divine plan and destiny for your life.

- you understand Jesus has already won the victory.

- you do things according to the will of God.

All that remains is for you to understand the will of God for your life, and then to walk in the victory that is yours through Jesus Christ.

What can you say to all these things? If God is for you, who can be against you? You can be the person God wants you to be. You can be victorious. You can go beyond the limits of the world and enter into the abundance of the kingdom of God. You can do all things through Christ who strengthens you!

Chapter Two

Triumphing Over Your Limits

After the Allies won World War II, the free world celebrated the defeat of the enemy. Military heroes were given ticker-tape parades. There was great rejoicing and dancing in the streets, along with many open displays of gratitude and thanksgiving. Good had triumphed over evil, and the war was finally over.

Celebrating triumph in war is an age-old practice. The Romans had great parades after the defeat of their enemies. In fact, the Greek word for "triumph" in the time of Christ was *thriambeuo*. It was the same word used for a parade in which the captured enemies of the Roman Empire were marched in front of thousands of cheering people. The Roman triumph was an ancient form of the ticker-tape parade.

Celebrating Victory Over the Enemy

The apostle Paul used the descriptive language of a military victory parade to describe Jesus' triumph over an evil enemy:

> *Having disarmed principalities and pow-*
> *ers, He made a public spectacle of them, tri-*
> *umphing [thriambeuo] over them in it.*
>
> (Colossians 2:15)

Jesus died, descended into hell, conquered death and the grave, and rose again. He defeated all the enemies of God and led a victory parade back to heaven. We can only try to imagine what this triumph must have been like. It was surely a greater triumph than any celebrated after any war waged by human beings against one other.

Jesus is still triumphant over the enemies of darkness. He has returned to heaven and is seated next to His heavenly Father. Remarkably, Jesus allows us to share in His triumph over God's enemy and ours—the devil.

> *Now thanks be to God who always leads*
> *us in triumph [thriambeuo] in Christ, and*
> *through us diffuses the fragrance of His*
> *knowledge in every place.*
>
> (2 Corinthians 2:14)

WE ARE TO SHARE IN JESUS' TRIUMPH AND BRING GLORY TO GOD THROUGH OUR WORDS AND ACTIONS.

Right now, Jesus allows us to join in His parade of triumph over the enemy. He enables us to live a life of faith and purpose in which we can demonstrate His victory and overcome limitations in our lives. We are to share in Jesus' triumph and bring glory to God through our words and actions. We are to make known the sweet smell of Jesus' triumph wherever we go.

Since Jesus has won the victory over the devil, we can appropriate the spoils of His triumph, by faith, as we need them. Grasp what this truth is all about, and you will realize what it means to live a life with no more limitations, in which heaven's blessings are unleashed.

KING DAVID'S MEN—FROM DISTRESS TO TRIUMPH

DAVID WAS VICTORIOUS OVER GOLIATH

Triumph is a theme that runs throughout the Bible. One of the best-known examples is the story of David and Goliath. David killed the Philistine giant with a stone from his slingshot. David's slingshot should not have brought down a heavily armored warrior, but God guided the stone right between the giant's eyes, so that he fell. David ran to Goliath, took his sword, and cut off his head. He then held up the head of Israel's enemy for everybody to see. With the help of God, he had triumphed completely over Goliath. (See 1 Samuel 17.)

David's triumphant display of the giant's head was a symbol of our victory over the devil. Jesus has defeated the "giant" devil, and we are no longer to be afraid of him. Jesus has chopped off his head. We need to learn what spiritual triumph really means and apply it to our daily lives. Our triumph in Christ means the devil cannot limit us any longer.

DISTRESSED, DISCONTENTED, AND IN DEBT

We can learn more about triumph by looking into the life of David and his men after David defeated Goliath. David's victory gave him great favor with the Israelites. He received King Saul's daughter as his wife, and he was given a good job working for the king. But his struggles were not over. The king became jealous of David's success and decided to kill him. King Saul's threats caused David to run for his life, and he ended up in a cave in the wilderness.

The following Scripture passage tells what happened next:

> *David therefore departed from there and escaped to the cave of Adullam. So when his brothers and all his father's house heard it, they went down there to him. And everyone who was in distress, everyone who was in debt, and everyone who was discontented gathered to him. So he became captain over them. And there were about four hundred men with him.* (1 Samuel 22:1–2)

Try to imagine this scenario. David is hiding in a cave, King Saul and his army are chasing him and trying to kill him, and David is surely crying out to God to help him. Whom does God send to him? People who are in debt, people who are in distress, and people who are discontented. All the people who were in counseling and therapy went to where David was, but that was not the worst of it. He became a captain over them.

God gave David men who may have looked like failures, but He had great plans for these four hundred men and their leader. David did not stay in trouble, and neither did his followers. David was a man after God's own heart. (See 1 Samuel 13:14.) He loved God. He also had great faith. All you have to do is read the many psalms David wrote to see how much he trusted and loved the Lord. God honored the faithfulness of David and eventually made him king instead of King Saul. God has a good plan for your life, too, so look to Him for your help, no matter how bad your situation may become.

TRANSFORMED INTO MIGHTY MEN

Read what the Bible has to say about David's men after David became the king of Israel.

These are the names of the mighty men whom David had: Josheb-Basshebeth the Tachmonite, chief among the captains. He was called Adino the Eznite, because he had killed eight hundred men at one time. And after him was Eleazar the son of Dodo, the Ahohite, one of the three mighty men with David when they defied the Philistines who were gathered there for battle, and the men of Israel had retreated. He arose and attacked the Philistines until his hand was weary, and his hand stuck to the sword. The LORD brought about a great victory that day; and the people returned after him only to plunder. And after him was Shammah the son of Agee the Hararite. The Philistines had gathered together into a troop where there was a piece of ground full of lentils. So the people fled from the Philistines. But

> *he stationed himself in the middle of the*
> *field, defended it, and killed the Philistines.*
> *So the* Lord *brought about a great victory.*
> (2 Samuel 23:8–12)

What a great transformation! In a few years' time, David's men went from being distressed, discontented, and in debt (and likely depressed as a result) to being honored as mighty men. They overcame the limitations of their circumstances and became triumphant, honored men in the service of King David. The above passage depicts David's followers not as weak men with limiting problems but as mighty men.

God helped David establish the nation of Israel as a powerful kingdom, so that David left a fortune for his son Solomon, who succeeded him. David ushered in an era that could be called Israel's "Golden Age." With God's help, he was able to triumph over his enemies and solidify a great kingdom that gave glory to God.

Change May Come over a Period of Time

David's success did not come all at once, however. He struggled for years before he triumphed over all his enemies. He killed Goliath while he was still a teenager, but he did not become king over all of Israel until he was thirty years old. (See 2 Samuel 5:4.)

It is good to remember that many changes do not occur overnight but over a period of time. It may take years before you triumph over some of the limitations in your life. Patience and continued diligence are important qualities to exercise while you are in the process of removing limits and overcoming obstacles.

David loved God tremendously, and it was his love for God that sustained him during his struggles. He is a good example for us to follow. Loving God and continuing to serve Him faithfully will ultimately cause you to triumph over your limits.

> LOVING GOD AND SERVING HIM FAITHFULLY WILL ULTIMATELY CAUSE YOU TO TRIUMPH OVER YOUR LIMITS.

THE FAITH HALL OF FAME

The exploits of King David and other great men and women of faith are recorded in the Bible to encourage you. The following verses from the book of Hebrews are part of what I like to call the Faith Hall of Fame:

> *And what more shall I say? For the time would fail me to tell of Gideon and Barak and Samson and Jephthah, also of David and Samuel and the prophets: who through faith subdued kingdoms, worked righteousness, obtained promises, stopped the mouths of lions, quenched the violence of fire, escaped the edge of the sword, out of weakness were made strong, became valiant in battle, turned to flight the armies of the aliens. Women received their dead raised to life again. Others were tortured, not accepting deliverance, that they might obtain a better resurrection. Still others had trial of mockings and scourgings, yes, and of chains and imprisonment. They were stoned, they were sawn in two, were tempted, were slain with*

the sword. They wandered about in sheep-
skins and goatskins, being destitute, af-
flicted, tormented; of whom the world was
not worthy. They wandered in deserts and
mountains, in dens and caves of the earth.
(Hebrews 11:32–38)

The heroes in the Faith Hall of Fame were humble heroes. Hebrews 11 describes how they glorified God by their great deeds. Through faith, they subdued kingdoms. They closed the mouths of lions. Out of weakness, they were made strong. They defeated armies and raised the dead. They were not afraid of death; some of them suffered and even died for their faith. They had the attitude, "You can kill me if you want to. I am not afraid of being stoned to death or sawn in half." The Bible concludes that the world was not worthy of such great heroes.

GOD HAS PROVIDED SOMETHING BETTER FOR US

And all these, having obtained a good tes-
timony through faith, did not receive the
promise, God having provided something
better for us, that they should not be made
perfect apart from us. (Hebrews 11:39–40)

These faith heroes did mighty things. However, their work will not be complete until we take God's promises and do mighty deeds, as well. They have to wait for us to finish the work of faith they started. We have to live lives of faith and bring glory to God, so that they will see the completion of their work.

What was the promise they did not receive? God told Abraham that his children and his children's children would be a blessing to the world. (See, for example, Genesis 22:16–18.) By faith, years before Jesus was born, Abraham "saw" that a day would arrive when one of his descendants would come to save the world. (See John 8:56.) Abraham and the other great men and women of faith in the Old Testament could not receive the promise of Jesus in their time. They could see Him only by faith.

Do you realize that you know more about Jesus than the people in the Old Testament did? In the New Testament, you have a written record, made by eyewitnesses, that tells you who Jesus Christ was and what He did. You also have wonderful, divinely inspired letters written by Jesus' apostles, as well as by other followers of Jesus, to the early churches. You have more information to work with than the people under the old covenant did.

These ancient witnesses "surround" us, as the book Hebrews describes it. They are still alive, existing in heaven. Someday, we will meet them, and we will be able to say we completed what they started. Because they have left us this tremendous testimony, we should desire to purify ourselves and to run the race of faith that is before us.

> *Therefore we also, since we are surrounded by so great a cloud of witnesses, let us lay aside every weight, and the sin which so easily ensnares us, and let us run with endurance the race that is set before us, looking unto Jesus, the author and finisher of our faith, who for the joy that was set before Him endured the cross, despising the shame, and has sat down at the right hand of the throne of God.* (Hebrews 12:1–2)

The heroes of faith are waiting for us to glorify God in our lives and to finish the work they started. We can do something they cannot. We can share the good news of Jesus with a dying world. This is the privilege we have been given. We live in a day that men and women from ancient times could only dream about. We live in the time of the risen, all-powerful Savior, who openly triumphed over the forces of evil!

YOU CAN TRIUMPH
OVER THE LIMITATIONS OF YOUR PAST

Because we live in the time of the risen Savior, we can triumph over the regrets and setbacks of our pasts. Many people are limiting themselves by memories of past failures. Why do you want to dwell on the memories of your past? You should forget the past. Think about the things God has put in front of you. Think about how you have been made to triumph in Jesus. Think about the calling of God on your life. Think about the wonderful things Jesus Christ has done for you.

Paul understood the importance of forgetting the past and looking forward to what God had called him to do. He wrote,

> *Brethren, I do not count myself to have apprehended; but one thing I do, forgetting those things which are behind and reaching forward to those things which are ahead, I press toward the goal for the prize of the upward call of God in Christ Jesus.*
> (Philippians 3:13–14)

Paul also gave advice on how to take control of thoughts that are contrary to the will of God:

Casting down arguments and every high thing that exalts itself against the knowledge of God, bringing every thought into captivity to the obedience of Christ.
(2 Corinthians 10:5)

You can replace thoughts of failure with thoughts of success. Living your life dwelling on past failures just reinforces the chances that you will fail again. Replace your old picture of failure and defeat with a new picture of success and victory.

> REPLACE YOUR OLD PICTURE OF FAILURE AND DEFEAT WITH A NEW PICTURE OF SUCCESS AND VICTORY.

God wants you to know you can triumph over the Goliaths in your life. You can fulfill your destiny. You can be an overcomer now. Jesus has done the work. He has already defeated the enemy. All you have to do is join in the victory parade. You can take your place next to the other great heroes of faith, walk in victory, and triumph over the limitations in your life.

REJOICE IN YOUR VICTORY!

At our church one night, God moved in a powerful way at the close of an intercessory prayer service. We began to rejoice and shout. We were not being foolish or crazy. We were just celebrating our victory in Jesus. We were triumphing over the enemy.

During this time of rejoicing, it became real to me that there are no more limits as to what we can do in God. This means that whatever situation you are facing—spiritual, emotional, financial, or physical—there are no more hindrances to hold you back. God's power and blessings are available to you. The choice is yours: You can live with your distress, discontentment, indebtedness, and depression, or you can become mighty in God.

You can and should live in triumph over the limitations in your life. You can do nothing in yourself, but you can do all things through Christ who strengthens you. (See Philippians 4:13.) There is no reason to fail. You can and should live a life of victory that brings glory to God. In Christ, you are free from the things that would prevent you from being all you can be. Enjoy your triumph in Christ. Rejoice in your victory!

CHAPTER THREE

ARE YOUR BLESSINGS BEING BLOCKED?

Years ago, when my wife, Jeanne, and I first started in the ministry, we would visit all kinds of prisons. Once, we visited a federal prison in Michigan, and we spent the night there. We slept in bedrolls on the gymnasium floor, with just a net to separate us from the prisoners. This was a wonderful experience, because we were able to talk to the prisoners one-on-one. Many of them were not Christians, and some of them wanted to find out about Christianity and change their lives.

The warden of this prison gave me some insight into how we form limitations in our minds. He said that prisons are institutions, and, after being there for years, the prisoners become institutionalized, meaning that they have established limits within themselves. Then, the warden added something I will never forget. He said that if they were to remove the fence, most of the guys would not want to leave. After spending years within its limitations, many of them had become so accustomed to living inside it that it would be hard for them to think about living in any other way.

The prison fence represented the boundary in their way of thinking; it limited how far they could go. If the physical barrier had been removed, the mental barrier still would have been there. Since they had been conditioned never to go beyond that boundary, they had become imprisoned in their minds.

Limitations are boundaries. Everyone struggles with some spiritual, mental, emotional, or physical boundary. We all have certain limiting circumstances and ways of thinking, so that limitations are a part of everyday life for us. When Jesus comes into our lives, He wants to remove the limits that are hindering us. We, however, are so used to the status quo that we find it hard to venture beyond our limitations. We are imprisoned in our minds.

GOOD LIMITS AND BAD LIMITS

> GOOD LIMITS KEEP US FROM HURTING OURSELVES. BAD LIMITS PREVENT US FROM EXPERIENCING GOD'S FULLNESS.

Let us first make a distinction between good limits and bad limits. Good limits keep us from living foolishly and hurting ourselves and others. Bad limits prevent us from experiencing the fullness of God in our lives.

So, when I say that we are no longer to accept limits in our lives, I am *not* advocating disobeying the laws of the land and other regulations that are necessary to keep our lives in order. I am not talking about living foolishly. I am not talking about going out and charging all your credit cards to the maximum or recklessly speeding down the highway.

Instead, I am referring to limits in our lives that keep God at a distance from us, limits that we have accepted but that are contrary to His will. These are bad limits, and they need to be removed.

How do bad limits keep us from experiencing the fullness of God? They prevent us from receiving healing in our bodies and wholeness in our souls and emotions, from entering into true worship, and from engaging in Christian service and helping others.

All of us must understand that we need to set good limits, exercising self-control in our spirits, minds, and bodies. The limitations we have to remove are those that have kept God from fulfilling His purposes and plans for our lives. He wants us to live lives that bring glory to Him and joy to us.

THINKING AND ACTING LIKE SLAVES

The historical accounts in the Scriptures are included for our instruction. Various books of the Bible show how God Himself was limited by the unbelief of the nation of Israel while the Israelites were traveling in the wilderness. These limitations grieved Him. (See Psalm 78:40–41.)

The Israelites had been slaves in Egypt for many years. Then, God used Moses to set them free, and He told them He would bring them into the Promised Land, the land of Canaan. Many mighty miracles were performed by God in the process of their deliverance. After the pharaoh of Egypt refused to let the Israelites go, the Egyptians were decimated with many plagues. Finally, the pharaoh agreed to let Moses take the Israelites away. (See Exodus 12:31–32.)

However, at the last minute, he changed his mind, and he set out with his army to stop them from leaving the country. But God had a different plan. Though His power, Moses parted the Red Sea, and the Israelites walked across on dry land. (See Exodus 14:21–22.) When the pharaoh and his army tried to follow them, the sea came back over them, and they all perished. (See verses 27–28.) This was a tremendous triumph for the Israelites, and they rejoiced in their victory over the enemy:

> *Then Moses and the children of Israel sang this song to the LORD, and spoke, saying: "I will sing to the LORD, for He has triumphed gloriously! The horse and its rider He has thrown into the sea!"*   (Exodus 15:1)

God continued to do great and mighty deeds for His people. He met their needs in the desert by making water flow from rocks, and causing food, which the people called "manna," to fall from heaven. (See Exodus 16:1–17:7; Numbers 20:7–13.) He gave them a pillar of cloud by day and a pillar of fire by night to lead them. (See Exodus 13:21–22.) God demonstrated His willingness to meet every need they had. They experienced miracles every day in the desert.

God had removed the Israelites from Egypt. He had delivered them from their enemies. Their needs were being met in the desert. They lived continually in the presence of God. They were no longer slaves under harsh taskmasters; they were free. However, they did not act like they were free. Even though they had been given all manner of blessings, they continued to *think* like slaves. Even though they had been physically liberated from slavery, they continued to *behave* like slaves. Therefore, they did not receive all the blessings God had intended for them. He had taken them out of Egypt, but He could not take Egypt out of them.

Almost all of the Israelites who had been slaves in Egypt never made it into the Promised Land because they rebelled against God when He was ready to bring them into that land, which was *"flowing with milk and honey"* (Exodus 3:8). As a consequence, they wandered in the desert for forty years, while they continued to rebel many times, until they had all died. God had intended for these ex-slaves to move forward as free people into the Promised Land, but their unbelief kept them from entering in to it.

LIVING OUTSIDE THE BORDER OF BLESSING

What happened to prevent these ex-slaves from living in the Promised Land? When they were on the border of Canaan, they saw heavily defended cities and giants in the land, and they became full of doubt, fear, and unbelief. They saw themselves as grasshoppers in comparison with the inhabitants. As a result, they rebelled against God and refused to take possession of their inheritance. (See Numbers 13–14.)

The Israelites quickly forgot how God had drowned the mightiest army in the world, the Egyptian army, on their behalf. They forgot how He had caused them to triumph over their enemies. They refused to believe they could take the land. They failed to realize that God was the One who was going to drive out the inhabitants of the land before them. All they had to do

IF THE ISRAELITES WHO HAD BEEN FREED FROM EGYPTIAN SLAVERY HAD OBEYED GOD, THEY WOULD HAVE ENTERED THE PROMISED LAND.

was believe and obey God, and they would have been allowed to live in their Promised Land.

Only two men had faith to believe they could possess the land: Joshua and Caleb. Of all the slaves who had left Egypt, they were the only two who were allowed into the Promised Land after the rest of the Israelites rebelled. (See Numbers 14:6–9, 24.) These two men were full of faith, and they lived to conquer and triumph over their enemies.

It was left to the children of the ex-slaves to possess the Promised Land. When these children grew up, and after their rebellious parents had died, God allowed them to leave the desert and take the land. (See Joshua 1:1–6; 5:2–7.) They had to fight for the Promised Land, but it was God who provided the victory. They went on to receive, by faith and obedience, the inheritance He had promised their parents.

LEARNING FROM ISRAEL'S EXAMPLE OF UNBELIEF

The following passage describes how the people of Israel worked against God's purposes while they were wandering in the desert.

How often they provoked Him in the wilderness, and grieved Him in the desert! Yes, again and again they tempted God, and limited the Holy One of Israel. They did not

*remember His power: the day when He re-
deemed them from the enemy, when He
worked His signs in Egypt, and His wonders in the field of Zoan.* (Psalm 78:40–43)

We can identify several ways in which the Israelites worked in opposition to God's purposes: they
(1) provoked Him, (2) grieved Him, (3) tempted Him,
(4) limited Him, and (5) did not remember how He
had miraculously saved them from slavery. Hebrews
3:17–19 says,

Now with whom was [God] *angry forty
years? Was it not with those who sinned,
whose corpses fell in the wilderness? And
to whom did He swear that they would
not enter His rest, but to those who did not
obey? So we see that they could not enter in
because of unbelief.*

Let us look more closely at the ways in which
the Israelites rebelled against God, and the conse-
quences of that rebellion. We can learn from their
negative example and not make the same mistakes
they did and miss the blessings God has in store
for us.

1. ISRAEL PROVOKED GOD

When Psalm 78 says the Israelites *"provoked"*
God, it refers to their rebellion against Him. Rebellion is an evil thing to God. First Samuel 15:23 says
that *"rebellion is as the sin of witchcraft."* Rebellion is
saying no when you should be saying yes. Rebellion
is stubbornly going against God when He is trying to
lead you forward.

God instructs us in many ways. He may use the truths and teachings we receive from reading the Bible, the leading of His Spirit, or the wisdom or knowledge of another person. He has provided pastors, evangelists, prophets, teachers, and apostles to help us. (See Ephesians 4:7–8, 11–16.) Whenever God tries to instruct or counsel you, and you rebel against Him, you are provoking Him.

When you rebel against God, you demonstrate unbelief. You are saying, in essence, that your way is better than God's way. You show that you do not trust God and His goodness. Rebellion is a lack of understanding of and appreciation for God's true love and concern for you. Rebellion upsets God and limits His ability to bless you.

2. Israel Grieved God

God is grieved when you do not have faith in His promises. You actually cause Him sorrow when you do not believe. He will make a way for you to receive His blessings, but your unbelief will limit Him. He is pleased when you believe and then act on your belief. He is grieved when you think and act contrary to faith. We cannot receive God's promises when we operate in unbelief. While our unbelief causes Him sorrow, our faith brings Him joy.

3. Israel Tempted God

Israel continually tried to tempt, or test, God. They would not believe Him when He spoke through Moses. They demanded that He prove Himself over and over again. God does not have to prove Himself.

Jesus was the perfect example of the unlimited potential of God, and He did not limit God by tempting Him.

> *Then the devil took* [Jesus] *up into the holy city, set Him on the pinnacle of the temple, and said to Him, "If You are the Son of God, throw Yourself down. For it is written: 'He shall give His angels charge over you,' and, 'In their hands they shall bear you up, lest you dash your foot against a stone.'" Jesus said to him, "It is written again, 'You shall not tempt the Lord your God.'"*
>
> (Matthew 4:5–7)

Jesus withstood the devil's temptations and would not fall for his tricks. In the above temptation, the devil quoted Scripture and told Jesus to throw Himself down from the top of the temple to prove to everybody that He was the Son of God. We tempt God when we misapply the Scriptures. The Scriptures were given for us to do the will of God, not the will of the devil or the will of human beings.

Jesus came to do the will of His heavenly Father, and He did not allow Himself to test God. He did not have to show off His powers to verify anything to the devil or anyone else. He was confident in who He was and in the purpose God had for Him. Jesus had faith in God and knew He needed to do only what His Father wanted Him to do. He used His power to suit God's purposes, not the devil's.

We must believe, by faith, that God will do what He says in His Word He will do. We should not need miraculous signs from God to have faith in Him.

> WE MUST BELIEVE, BY FAITH, THAT GOD WILL DO WHAT HE SAYS IN HIS WORD HE WILL DO.

Jesus taught that an evil generation seeks miraculous signs. (See Matthew 12:39.) Many people ask for signs as proofs of certain things. When you ask God for miraculous signs to help you believe, you are tempting Him. Belief does not need miraculous signs.

Instead, such signs should be a *product* of faith. We should have signs following our faith, not preceding it. (See Mark 16:17–18.) When you reverse the order and require a sign first in order to believe, you are tempting God. Most people have it backward. The proper order is that belief comes first, and then miracles happen.

4. ISRAEL LIMITED GOD

Because the Israelites did not believe God, they turned away from His plan for them to enter the Promised Land. Anytime you turn back from your forward motion in the direction God is leading you, you limit Him.

The apostle Paul told the Galatians that he was concerned for them because they had turned back to bondage after they had come to know freedom in God. Jesus had shown them a new way to live. Yet, instead of trusting in Jesus and moving forward in their freedom, they turned back to the dead elements of religious bondage.

> *But now after you have known God, or rather are known by God, how is it that you turn again to the weak and beggarly*

elements, to which you desire again to be in bondage? You observe days and months and seasons and years. I am afraid for you, lest I have labored for you in vain.
                                        (Galatians 4:9–11)

Religious bondage, which I will talk more about in the next chapter, is a product of man's desire to control people through legalism. God had set the Galatians free from religious legalism (see Galatians 5:1), yet they had decided to turn back to it. Once you are free from the things that had you bound, turning back to them is never acceptable, and it will only limit God from working in your life.

Jesus told His disciples that no one is fit for the kingdom of God if he turns back after having put his hand to the plow. (See Luke 9:62.) Another term for "turning back" is *backsliding.* You limit God when you backslide by returning to a life of disobedience to Him.

What lies ahead for us as believers is much greater than anything we have left behind—or will leave behind, as God leads us. One of the devil's tricks is to try to convince you that your best days were in your past. The truth is that your best days lie ahead.

5. ISRAEL DID NOT REMEMBER GOD'S POWER

God performed many signs for the Israelites, but they still did not remember what He had done for them. They had forgotten how He had miraculously delivered them from the Egyptians.

Let us not forget what God has done for us! Do you remember when you were lost? Do you remember when your thoughts, attitudes, and actions were predominantly contrary to God's nature? Do you remember when church was the furthest thing from your mind? If you have been delivered from much, you ought to be grateful for much. You should remember and be thankful to God.

When you forget where you were before Jesus came into your life, you limit God. You must recall what you were saved from and who saved you. Remember the One who brought you out of your lostness. Remember the One who delivered you from Satan and sin. Remember the One who healed you. Remember everything Jesus has already done for you.

Sometimes, it is easy to lose sight of what God has accomplished for us. When we come across a little problem, trial, or obstacle, we soon forget all the ways He has worked in our lives.

> REMINDING OURSELVES OF GOD'S GOODNESS AND FAITHFULNESS TO US IN THE PAST HELPS US TO HAVE FAITH IN HIM FOR THE PRESENT.

Reminding ourselves of His goodness and faithfulness to us in the past helps us to have faith in Him for the present. We must realize that He never changes; He is the same God He always has been. (See James 1:17; Hebrews 13:8.) We are the ones who need to change.

FAITH IN GOD RELEASES YOU FROM LIMITATIONS

By faith, you have been born again. By faith, you have been set free from the bondage and limitations of the devil. By faith, you have been made more than a conqueror through Jesus Christ. By faith, you can do all things through Christ who strengthens you. Faith in God and His promises is the answer for rebellion and turning back. Faith in God releases you from the grip of unbelief and takes you into new territory. Faith in God allows you to receive from God all He has planned for you.

Unfortunately, many people never receive everything God has planned for them. Not unlike the former Egyptian slaves, they fail to accept the blessings that God wants them to have. They do not appropriate these blessings by faith, and therefore they do not partake of the best He has for them.

The Israelites who died in the wilderness limited God. It was not His intention for them to die in the wilderness. He wanted them to believe and trust in Him. He wanted them to enjoy the Promised Land. Sadly, they rebelled against Him and died without entering in. We need to consider these things and avoid being left in our own wildernesses. Their example has been given to us so that we can have faith in God and not limit Him through unbelief. Walking in faith helps you to enter in to God's Promised Land of unlimited potential.

Chapter Four

Freedom from the Limits of Religious Tradition

I received a letter from a woman who was confused by a TV preacher who had said that God puts sickness and disease on people to teach them something. She had thought that God wanted her to be healthy, and she had believed God for her healing. But this preacher had put doubt in her mind when he said, "God uses the devil to teach His children lessons."

The woman could not understand why God would want the devil to make her sick. If He was using the devil, what was she supposed to be learning? She was sick and tired of being sick and tired. She wanted to know if I thought God had sent the devil to teach her something, and if I thought God might not want her healed.

I knew I had to use wisdom in how I answered this woman because she was bedridden. I knew her life might be at stake. She was at risk of dying at an early age, and I needed to answer her carefully according to God's Word. So, I began by telling her, "Since you asked me, let's look at what the Word says. You have to look at the whole Bible to understand what God is doing, and God does not use evil to tempt His children."

Then, I told her to read James 1:13–17. This Scripture passage plainly says that God does not use evil to accomplish His purposes. I said to her, "God did not send the devil to teach you a lesson. God wants to heal you."

> *Let no one say when he is tempted, "I am tempted by God"; for God cannot be tempted by evil, nor does He Himself tempt anyone.*
> (James 1:13)

We have seen that another word for tempting is *testing*. God is not tested by evil, and He does not test anyone with evil circumstances. That would contradict His nature.

I have seen many people who were in bad shape from cancer and other illnesses. Sickness and disease are evil things. Anybody who says sickness or disease is something good has never spent time in the hospital praying for sick people. Sickness and disease destroy lives and kill people.

I have a difficult time believing God wants anyone to be sick. Jesus came to show us how to have abundant life. (See John 10:10.) Abundant life must include health, and I believe sickness and disease are limitations from which Jesus can set us free.

JESUS CARRIED YOUR SICKNESSES AND PAINS

The topic of healing has been controversial among various churches and denominations for a long time. Many people do not believe God still heals today.

This is a subject to which I have given much thought. I believe many people are limiting God in the area of healing because of their religious traditions. They will gladly teach that *spiritual* healing is for today, but they will stop short of saying *physical* healing is for today.

HEALING IS PART OF REDEMPTION

It is God's will to heal you physically just as much as it is His will to heal you spiritually. Jesus' death on the cross paid the price to redeem humanity from sin. His death settled the sin issue and made a way for us to receive access to the favor of God, and I believe physical healing is part of God's plan of redemption.

> IT IS GOD'S WILL TO HEAL YOU PHYSICALLY JUST AS MUCH AS IT IS HIS WILL TO HEAL YOU SPIRITUALLY.

Jesus' death on the cross was physical. When you deny that physical healing is part of redemption, you are limiting God, and you are not properly discerning the Lord's body or His blood, which was shed for you.

When we take Communion, the bread and the wine or grape juice are symbolic of the body and blood of Jesus. The apostle Paul said many believers in the Corinthian church did not properly discern the body of Christ, which had been broken for them, and so they became sick and died.

But let a man examine himself, and so let him eat of the bread and drink of the cup.

> *For he who eats and drinks in an unworthy manner eats and drinks judgment to himself, not discerning the Lord's body. For this reason many are weak and sick among you, and many sleep.*
>
> (1 Corinthians 11:28–30)

The apostle Peter included healing along with the forgiveness of sins in his discussion of redemption through Christ. He said the broken body of Jesus was for our healing, mentioning that the bloody marks Jesus bore from being whipped were proof of our healing.

> [Jesus] *Himself bore our sins in His own body on the tree, that we, having died to sins, might live for righteousness; by whose stripes you were healed.* (1 Peter 2:24)

Peter's statement was based on a passage from the book of Isaiah. This Scripture gives us a picture of the suffering Jesus endured for us:

> *Surely He has borne our griefs and carried our sorrows; yet we esteemed Him stricken, smitten by God, and afflicted. But He was wounded for our transgressions, He was bruised for our iniquities; the chastisement for our peace was upon Him, and by His stripes we are healed.* (Isaiah 53:4–5)

It is interesting to note what tense Isaiah used when speaking of healing. He used the present tense: "*by His stripes we* **are** *healed.*" Isaiah was looking forward prophetically to Jesus' death. Then, in

1 Peter 2:24, Peter used the past tense when he said, "*By whose stripes you **were** healed.*" He was looking *back* to the cross. Let us understand this very important point: The death of Jesus on the cross is the focal point of the Bible. Everything in the Bible points to the moment when humanity was redeemed from sin, sickness, disease, poverty, and death.

The prophet Isaiah said Jesus bore our griefs and carried our sorrows. The Hebrew word for "griefs" is *choliy*. This word is translated as "*grief*" or "*griefs*" four times in the Old Testament, but, in other places in the Old Testament, it is translated as "*sickness*" or "*sicknesses*" (twelve times) and "*disease*" (seven times). The Hebrew word for "*sorrows*" is *makob*. This same word is also translated as "*pain*" in two other places in the Old Testament. It can mean either physical or mental pain.

Where the book of Isaiah says, "*He has borne our griefs and carried our sorrows,*" it would not be inappropriate to read it as, "Jesus bore our sicknesses, our diseases, and our mental and physical pains." Personalize this truth and repeat it to yourself. Say, "When Jesus died on the cross, He bore my sicknesses and carried my pains."

Life Forever and Healing for the Present

Let's look at another example in the Bible that shows Jesus died for our healing. When talking about His eventual death on the cross, Jesus reminded His followers of the time when, under God's instruction, Moses put a replica of a snake on a pole and the Israelites were physically healed when they looked at it. The following is what happened: While they were wandering in the desert, the Israelites began complaining about their lack of food and water. *"Fiery serpents"* (Numbers 21:6) began to attack them, and many of the people were dying from their snakebites. God told Moses to make a brass serpent and put it on a pole. Those who had been bitten by the snakes could look at the serpent on the pole and live. (See verses 4–9.)

This serpent on the pole was symbolic of Jesus on the cross:

> *As Moses lifted up the serpent in the wilderness, even so must the Son of Man be lifted up, that whoever believes in Him should not perish but have eternal life. For God so loved the world that He gave His only begotten Son, that whoever believes in Him should not perish but have everlasting life. For God did not send His Son into the world to condemn the world, but that the world through Him might be saved.*
>
> (John 3:14–17)

Healing is part of redemption. Jesus, who knew no sin, was made to be sin for us, so that we might have God's righteousness through Him. (See 2 Corinthians 5:21.) Our righteousness in Christ entitles us to live forever and to have healing for the present.

JESUS DEMONSTRATED GOD'S WILL CONCERNING HEALING

Jesus showed us God's will for our healing not only through His death, but also through His life.

God the Father sent Jesus, His Son, to demonstrate love to the world. Jesus was God's love in action; He said that to see Him was to see the Father. (See John 14:9.) With many signs and wonders, He demonstrated God's ability and willingness to heal.

The Bible records no instance when Jesus sent someone away until that person had suffered enough and learned his or her lesson. Instead, it clearly records Jesus doing many mighty healing miracles. He had power over all sicknesses and diseases.

> *Then Jesus went about all the cities and villages, teaching in their synagogues, preaching the gospel of the kingdom, and healing every sickness and every disease among the people.* (Matthew 9:35)

The above verse does not say He healed just a few every now and then. It says He healed *"every sickness and every disease."* Jesus demonstrated that He was a healing Savior. There were no limitations on His ability and willingness to heal.

When Jesus was arrested by the men who would take Him away to be crucified, Peter used his sword to cut off the ear of one of them. Even then, when being led away to die, Jesus healed the man's ear. (See Luke 22:50–51.)

I find it hard to imagine Jesus doing anything other than healing people. To say Jesus puts sickness on people to teach them something goes against everything you read about Him in the Bible. This type of thinking is based on religious traditions that deny the ability of God to work in our lives today.

Seek Healing When You Need It

The Bible tells us to seek help when we are sick. People who teach that healing is not for today must have to go to great lengths to explain away the following Scripture passage:

> *Is anyone among you sick? Let him call for the elders of the church, and let them pray over him, anointing him with oil in the name of the Lord. And the prayer of faith will save the sick, and the Lord will raise him up. And if he has committed sins, he will be forgiven.* (James 5:14–15)

> **Instead of establishing traditions in our churches *against* healing, we should have traditions *for* healing.**

Instead of establishing traditions in our churches *against* healing, we should have traditions *for* healing. The tradition in the early church was to have the elders anoint the sick with oil and pray for them. When the sick were prayed for, they were healed. If they had sinned, they were forgiven at the same time.

If God wanted some people to be sick, why would the apostle James have written the above passage? He said that if there is *"anyone among you sick,"* God will heal him, if he is anointed with oil and prayed for in faith.

It seems as if James expected all the sick people in the church to be healed. He did not question whether it was God's will. He did not say to let people stay sick a little longer so they could learn a lesson. He said the prayer of faith would save the sick. It is always God's will to heal those who come before the church and petition for healing.

DISTINGUISH GOOD TRADITIONS FROM BAD TRADITIONS

Just as not all limits are bad, not all religious traditions are bad. The traditions of baptism and Communion are good. These traditions are clearly outlined in the Bible. Religious traditions that are bad are those that hinder the power of God in the lives of people. Many man-made traditions are based upon wrong beliefs. These traditions teach you to settle for the tradition instead of believing in the fullness and richness of God and His Word.

For example, when someone says healing is not for today, or that it might not be God's will to heal you now, that is a bad tradition. If people are taught not to expect God to heal or bless them, then they are being indoctrinated with beliefs that can limit God from working in their lives. In the case of healing, it can literally be a matter of life and death. Rotten tradition can rob people of the lifesaving, healing power of God.

Many worthless traditions come from people misunderstanding the nature and character of God. God is always good. He is not the source of your problems. He is always the answer to your problems. Sin, sickness, disease, poverty, and death are problems that exist in this fallen world. Yet Jesus overcame all of them. He pointed out that He was the source of abundant life. He contrasted His purpose to the purpose of the devil when He said,

> *The thief does not come except to steal, and to kill, and to destroy. I have come that they may have life, and that they may have it more abundantly.* (John 10:10)

There is a real devil who causes real, significant problems on the earth. Satan is a spiritual outlaw. Jesus identified him as the source of crime and destruction. He said the devil comes to steal, kill, and destroy.

Many people who are caught up in bad religious traditions totally ignore the truth about the devil. Like the TV preacher whom I mentioned at the beginning of the chapter, they say that both good and evil come from God, and that the devil is just a tool used by God to beat His children into submission. Hurricanes, floods, tornadoes—these are all called "acts of God." Insurance companies use this term, and many religious people agree with it. Some of these people even consider the death of a loved one from cancer to be an act of God.

Traditions that attribute evil circumstances to God are worthless because they do not cause people to have faith in Him. Instead, they teach people to fear God in the wrong way and for the wrong reasons. The "fear" of God that the Bible encourages is an attitude of awe. (See, for example, Psalm 22:23–25; 33:8.) We should have reverence and respect for God, but we should not be afraid to ask Him for help when we need it. God does not want us to base our religion on fear. He wants us to base our religion on faith. It pleases Him when we have faith. Again, unbelief and fear impose limits on Him.

Traditions that are not based on faith but on fear will always put limitations on people. God does not want you to be hindered by fear. He wants you to be able to approach Him and to receive the good things you need for your life. You always need to approach God with the attitude that He is good and wants to bless you with good things.

> **GOD WANTS YOU TO BE ABLE TO APPROACH HIM AND TO RECEIVE THE GOOD THINGS YOU NEED FOR YOUR LIFE.**

If you then, being evil, know how to give good gifts to your children, how much more will your Father who is in heaven give good things to those who ask Him!

(Matthew 7:11)

Your heavenly Father is a loving Father. He is not a child abuser. He is not a criminal. If God were to be put on trial and convicted of all the crimes He has been accused of committing against His people, He would be sentenced to millions of years in prison! However, these accusations reveal a terrible misconception about God. The truth is that God is *good*, and He will not send evil on His children.

Your heavenly Father wants to provide good things to you as His child. He does not want you to be deprived of the things you need. He wants to give you many gifts. Most human parents desire only the best for their children, yet God's desire is even stronger to provide the best for His children.

Receive Limitless Life in Jesus

While Jesus ministered on earth, He was unlimited; He had spiritual power through the Holy Spirit. Yet the religious leaders of His day were limited; they did not operate in the power of God's Spirit.

Jesus demonstrated His power with many signs and wonders. He was able to show by example that God is willing to help people in their time of need. He revealed to us the will of God and showed us what it is like to live without limits. He was a living illustration that there are no financial limits, physical limits, emotional limits, or spiritual limits that cannot be overcome by the power of God.

Power Over Financial Limits

For example, Jesus had power to demonstrate the abundance of God over financial lack. He turned water into wine when the wine ran out at a wedding. (See John 2:1–11.) He blessed a struggling fishing business with so many fish that the fishermen's nets broke. (See Luke 5:1–11.) He turned the limited resources of a few loaves and fishes into an unlimited supply of food to feed a multitude. (See, for example, Mark 6:32–44.) He even found creative ways to satisfy the tax collector. Jesus sent Peter fishing, and the first fish he caught had a gold coin in its mouth, which was enough to pay the taxes for both Jesus and himself. (See Matthew 17:24–27.) And Jesus assured us that we could experience the same power over financial limits.

> *Do not seek what you should eat or what you should drink, nor have an anxious mind. For all these things the nations of the world seek after, and your Father knows that you need these things. But seek the kingdom of God, and all these things shall be added to you. Do not fear, little flock, for it is your Father's good pleasure to give you the kingdom.* (Luke 12:29–32)

POWER OVER THE LIMITS OF SICKNESS AND BONDAGE

Jesus also demonstrated the provision of God for healing and deliverance. No sickness or disease could prevail over His authority. He healed and delivered sick children from the oppression of the devil. (See, for example, Mark 7:24–30; Mark 9:14–29; John 4:46–54.) He opened blind eyes and healed lame limbs. (See, for example, Matthew 9:27–31; Mark 3:1–6; Luke 13:10–17; John 9:1–41.) On several occasions, He raised to life those who had died before their times. (See Luke 7:11–17; Matthew 9:18–19, 23–26; John 11:1–15.) And He said this same power and provision is available to us:

> *Most assuredly, I say to you, he who believes in Me, the works that I do he will do also; and greater works than these he will do, because I go to My Father. And whatever you ask in My name, that I will do, that*

the Father may be glorified in the Son.
(John 14:12–13)

POWER OVER EMOTIONAL LIMITS

Jesus demonstrated power over emotional limitations, and He openly showed that God deeply cares about our grief and pain. He had compassion on the widow of Nain who mourned the loss of her only son. Similarly, He was emotionally moved at the death of Lazarus. The Scriptures say that when He saw Lazarus' sister Mary and others weeping, *"He groaned in the spirit and was troubled"* (John 11:33), and then He Himself wept. (See verse 35). He raised both the widow's son and Lazarus from the dead, restoring them to their grieving family members. (See Luke 7:11–15; John 11:30–44.) Jesus also brought restoration from shame and forgiveness from guilt to the woman at the well, who'd had five husbands and was a social outcast, and to the woman caught in adultery. (See John 4:4–39; 8:10–11.) And He still assures us that His power is greater than our emotional limitations today:

> *Come to Me, all you who labor and are heavy laden, and I will give you rest. Take My yoke upon you and learn from Me, for I am gentle and lowly in heart, and you will find rest for your souls. For My yoke is easy and My burden is light.*
> (Matthew 11:28–30)

POWER OVER SPIRITUAL LIMITS

Our Savior demonstrated that He had power over spiritual limits when He rejected the temptations of the devil in the wilderness by the authority of the Word of God. The first Adam had succumbed to the temptation of the enemy, but Jesus overcame Satan. (See Matthew 4:1–11.) He also showed the effectiveness of prayer and the power of God over our spiritual limitations when He told Simon Peter, *"Simon, Simon! Indeed, Satan has asked for you, that he may sift you as wheat. But I have prayed for you, that your faith should not fail; and when you have returned to Me, strengthen your brethren"* (Luke 22:31–32). The Scriptures assure us that we can and will triumph over the spiritual limitations that came upon humanity when the first human begins rebelled against God in the garden of Eden. The apostle Paul wrote,

> *The first man was of the earth, made of dust; the second Man is the Lord from heaven. As was the man of dust, so also are those who are made of dust; and as is the heavenly Man, so also are those who are heavenly. And as we have borne the image of the man of dust, we shall also bear the image of the heavenly Man.* (1 Corinthians 15:47–49)

Jesus was the ultimate example of a Man operating by the power of God to overcome all limiting situations, and He is the example for us to follow. He came to show us how to live our lives to give glory to God.

Worthless religious traditions are dark and void of any real solutions to life's problems. Again, the religious leaders of Jesus' day offered no answers through their man-made traditions. Their religion was shallow and powerless, while Jesus' faith was deep and powerful. Jesus offered real solutions to

JESUS OFFERED REAL SOLUTIONS TO THE NEEDS OF PEOPLE THROUGH THE POWER OF THE HOLY SPIRIT.

the needs of people through the power of the Holy Spirit. The life He offered overcame all the limits of religious tradition. He was a bright light shining in the darkness.

Jesus scolded the religious leaders for taking the power out of the Word of God through their hollow traditions. He said to them, "[You make] *the word of God of no effect through your tradition which you have handed down. And many such things you do*" (Mark 7:13).

Worthless traditions often act as limitations where the promises of God are concerned. If God promises something in the Bible, we should never question whether it is His will. If He promises something, it is available to all who believe. This principle applies to salvation, healing, prosperity, or anything else you may need. If there is a promise in the Bible, and you have faith to believe it applies to you, then you can receive what you need from God.

In contrast, if you have been acting on the worthless traditions of men, you have limited the power of God in your life. Many people have been taught religiously week after week that God brings sickness and disease, or that God takes babies prematurely because He needs them to "brighten heaven." They have been taught that healing is not for today, the time for miracles has passed, and God does not work in the same way now that He did in the Gospels and the book of Acts.

Yes, traditions that are not based on sound knowledge and understanding of the will and the Word of God act as hindrances in many people's lives. These traditions become boundaries preventing them from experiencing the goodness and mercy of God. These limits must be broken before people can receive all God has for them.

THE TRUTH WILL FREE YOU FROM RELIGIOUS TRADITION

Jesus said, in effect, that if you continue to study the Word of God and apply it in your life, you will begin to know truth, and truth will set you free.

> *Then Jesus said to those Jews who believed Him, "If you abide in My word, you are My disciples indeed. And you shall know the truth, and the truth shall make you free."*
> (John 8:31–32)

The truth about God is what will set you free from religious and traditional limitations, which are based on wrong conceptions and beliefs about Him and the way He works.

> *But be doers of the word, and not hearers only, deceiving yourselves. For if anyone is a hearer of the word and not a doer, he is like a man observing his natural face in a mirror; for he observes himself, goes away, and immediately forgets what kind of man he was. But he who looks into the perfect law of liberty and continues in it, and is not*

a forgetful hearer but a doer of the work, this one will be blessed in what he does.
                                        (James 1:22–25)

James called the Word of God "*the perfect law of liberty.*" The Word of God will liberate you from the limitations imposed on you by worthless religious traditions.

DO NOT SETTLE
FOR THE LIMITATIONS OF TRADITION

In light of the above truths, do not settle for religious traditions that bring limitations into your life. People who are more than conquerors and triumphant in Christ should never compromise by accepting ideas that hinder their faith. Reject man-made traditions that keep God from operating on your behalf. Receive the fullness of God and His richness in every area of your life. Do not be content with the empty commandments of men. These are poor substitutes for the freedom found in a true relationship with the living, loving God.

> RECEIVE THE FULLNESS OF GOD AND HIS RICHNESS IN EVERY AREA OF YOUR LIFE.

Why would anyone choose hollow commandments over the freedom of God's Word? Pride and arrogance lead people to give man-made traditions and doctrines a high place in their lives. Jesus said these works are a vain attempt at worshipping God. Quoting the prophet Isaiah, He said to the religious leaders,

"In vain they worship Me, teaching as doctrines the commandments of men."...He said to them, "All too well you reject the commandment of God, that you may keep your tradition."   (Mark 7:7, 9)

Many religious leaders today also have a higher regard for their own vain traditions than they do for the Word of God. Their lives are devoid of God's power, and they teach others to be like themselves. Vain traditions...

- strangle the Word of God.
- explain away the power behind God's miracles.
- prevent people from expecting miracles to happen.
- rob people from receiving their blessings from God.
- interfere with true worship and fellowship with God.

JESUS TRIUMPHED OVER THE LIMITS OF RELIGIOUS TRADITION

Jesus had compassion on sinners, gently leading them to see the truth. He came to show us that everyone is a sinner and that we can find salvation through Him alone. Only through following Him and obeying His words can we live free from the limitations of religious tradition. On the other hand, Jesus expressed wrath and anger toward the religious hypocrites. He was quite outspoken against the established religious leaders of His day. He openly rebuked them, calling them *"whitewashed tombs which indeed appear beautiful outwardly, but inside are full of dead men's bones and all uncleanness"* (Matthew 23:27).

Jesus exposed the powerlessness of religious tradition, and this is why religious hypocrites hated Him. They plotted to hinder His work and to kill Him. Eventually, they put Jesus on trial and brought about His death on the cross. After He was crucified, they thought it was over. They were wrong. God raised Jesus from the dead, and their troubles were multiplied. Jesus sent forth His disciples in His name throughout the world with the message of hope and salvation. Jesus' resurrection was the ultimate triumph over the limitations of dead religion and useless traditions!

CHAPTER FIVE

RESTORING GOD'S BLESSINGS IN YOUR LIFE

The book of Job in the Old Testament describes a man who experienced great suffering but faced and overcame his severe hardships. He was a wealthy family man who lost almost everything he valued. He lost his children, he lost his financial security, and he lost his health. He struggled in the midst of these losses and attempted to understand his sufferings. In the end, he was restored by God; he regained his physical health and prosperity and started a new family that was a great blessing to him.

THE LIFE OF JOB: A STORY OF TRIUMPH BY GOD'S GRACE

Many people emphasize the sufferings of Job. The emphasis should not be on Job's sufferings but on his victory and triumph over his limiting circumstances. The book of Job is a wonderful story about a man's triumph over overwhelming adversity by God's grace.

JOB WAS A GOOD MAN

Many people think bad things do not happen to good people. Yet life does not work that way. Many times, bad things do happen to good people. Job was the best man on earth during his day. Read what God said about him:

> *Then the Lord said to Satan, "Have you con-*
> *sidered My servant Job, that there is none*
> *like him on the earth, a blameless and up-*
> *right man, one who fears God and shuns*
> *evil?"*   (Job 1:8)

God gave Job a great character reference. He said he was an *"upright man"* who reverenced Him and hated evil. God was not angry at Job. He considered Job a good man.

Job Had a Spiritual Enemy

Unfortunately, Job did not know he had an accuser working against him. (See Revelation 12:10.) He could not see the spiritual enemy who was about to attack him. Satan, or the devil, opposes everything good, and he came into Job's life to steal, kill, and destroy.

Satan began by denouncing Job before God. (See Job 1:9–11.) God acknowledged the devil's right to steal, kill, and destroy as the (temporary) *"god of this world"* (2 Corinthians 4:4 KJV). However, the Lord never changed His faithful confession about Job.

> *And the Lord said to Satan, "Behold, all*
> *that he has is in your power; only do not lay*
> *a hand on his person." So Satan went out*
> *from the presence of the Lord.*   (Job 1:12)

After Satan left God's presence, Job found himself in the middle of tremendous turmoil. Raiders stole his oxen and donkeys, and they killed all but one of the servants who were overseeing them. At the same time, other raiders came and stole his camels, killing all but one of the servants. A lightning storm killed all his sheep and all but one of the shepherds who were tending them. A tornado struck and killed all his sons and daughters while they were having a party. (See verses 13–19.)

Job Wrongly Blamed God for His Problems

Job did not know that Satan had the power to attack him. He did not have the advantage, as we do, of reading the book of Job and seeing behind the scenes. He thought God was the source of his distress and did not understand that the devil was the force behind the death and destruction.

Because Job did not know any better, he attributed his problems to God. The following passage describes his reaction after he suffered his great losses:

> Then Job arose, tore his robe, and shaved his head; and he fell to the ground and worshipped. And he said: "Naked I came from my mother's womb, and naked shall I return there. The Lord gave, and the Lord has taken away; blessed be the name of the Lord." In all this Job did not sin nor charge God with wrong. (Job 1:20–22)

Although Job thought God had taken his children and his wealth from him, this was not true. The death and destruction were the result of Satan's attacks. Note that this verse said Job had not sinned or charged God foolishly. He was not held accountable for not knowing who had come to steal, kill, and destroy in his life.

Then, Job's problems became even worse. After he'd lost his children, servants, and possessions, the devil once again accused him before God, and God allowed the devil to afflict Job's body but not kill him. Job developed painful sores from his head to his toes. (See Job 2:1–8.) His wife even wanted him to die.

> *Then his wife said to him, "Do you still hold fast to your integrity? Curse God and die!" But he said to her, "You speak as one of the foolish women speaks. Shall we indeed accept good from God, and shall we not accept adversity?" In all this Job did not sin with his lips.* (verses 9–10)

Again, Job's statements were untrue concerning God, although he did not realize it. (See James 1:13–17.) He entered into a time of deep despair. His friends came and tried to help him, but they did not know any more about the cause of his problems than he did.

JOB'S FRIENDS WRONGFULLY CONDEMNED HIM

Job's friends believed he had committed some terrible sin and that his tribulations were God's punishment for it. They tried to convince him that his sufferings had been brought about because of his wickedness. (See, for example, Job 4:7–9.) This could not have been further from the truth. Remember that God was pleased with Job. He was not angry at him. Job was a great example of a decent human being. His friends never won their case against Job, and God eventually rebuked them for not speaking correctly.

> And so it was, after the LORD had spoken these words to Job, that the LORD said to Eliphaz the Temanite, "My wrath is aroused against you and your two friends, for you have not spoken of Me what is right, as My servant Job has." (Job 42:7)

God then instructed them to make an offering to Him and to ask Job to pray for them.

> [The Lord said,] "Now therefore, take for yourselves seven bulls and seven rams, go to My servant Job, and offer up for yourselves a burnt offering; and My servant Job shall pray for you. For I will accept him, lest I deal with you according to your folly; because you have not spoken of Me what is right, as My servant Job has." So Eliphaz the Temanite and Bildad the Shuhite and Zophar the Naamathite went and did as the Lord commanded them; for the LORD had accepted Job. (verses 8–9)

God does not punish people for their sins by inflicting them with sickness and poverty. He does not punish people by killing their loved ones. He became angry at Job's friends when they claimed He was punishing Job with disease, poverty, and the death of his children and servants. Likewise, God is not pleased when we attribute death, disease, and destruction to Him. He is good and not evil. Job's friends did not correctly perceive the source of Job's problems, and God would not forgive their sins and accept them until they had made an offering to Him and Job had prayed for them.

How Job Triumphed Over His Limitations

By Faith and Grace

Job was one of the finest men ever born. Therefore, if his suffering was not the result of any sinful actions, what was his problem?

Job actually had two big problems. The first was that he did not operate in faith concerning his family and business. Job did not have great faith at this point in his life. He was in despair and admitted that what had happened to him was something he had "*greatly feared*":

> *For the thing I greatly feared has come upon me, and what I dreaded has happened to me.* (Job 3:25)

Fear does not overcome the world. In the absence of faith, great fear brings defeat. Job needed to overcome his fear and obtain faith to receive victory over the adverse circumstances in his life.

Job's second big problem was that he thought he could be made righteous by his good deeds. He didn't understand that no person, no matter how good, can be righteous by earning points for doing good things. Everyone must be made righteous by God's provision alone. He gives righteousness to everyone as a free gift. Salvation comes by the grace of God and is received by faith. (See Ephesians 2:8.)

Job needed faith and grace to triumph over his terrible circumstances. He could not overcome his problems without the help of God, and he needed to hear from God to find the faith and grace necessary to overcome his limitations.

> JOB NEEDED TO OVERCOME HIS FEAR AND OBTAIN FAITH TO RECEIVE VICTORY OVER THE ADVERSE CIRCUMSTANCES IN HIS LIFE.

BY HEARING GOD'S WORD

God was not the cause of Job's sufferings, and He never abandoned Job in the midst of them. God was the answer to his turmoil. He knew Job was in trouble; He hears the cries of those who are suffering. (See, for example, Psalm 34:17.) We have seen that Job needed to have faith in God. In the book of Romans, the apostle Paul explained that faith for salvation comes by hearing the Word of God.

For "whoever calls on the name of the LORD shall be saved." How then shall they call on Him in whom they have not believed? And how shall they believe in Him of whom they have not heard? And how shall they hear without a preacher? And how shall they preach unless they are sent? As it is written: "How beautiful are the feet of those who preach the gospel of peace, who bring glad tidings of good things!" But they have not all obeyed the gospel. For Isaiah says,

> *"Lᴏʀᴅ, who has believed our report?" So then faith comes by hearing, and hearing by the word of God.* (Romans 10:13–17)

Faith comes by hearing the Word of God. Job needed to hear God's voice to be saved from his terrible circumstances, and God spoke to him from the midst of a mighty windstorm.

> *Then the Lᴏʀᴅ answered Job out of the whirlwind, and said: "Who is this who darkens counsel by words without knowledge? Now prepare yourself like a man; I will question you, and you shall answer Me."*
> (Job 38:1–3)

God did not have to answer Job's accusations against Him. He said Job did not know what he was talking about. Job had tried to blame God for his circumstances, but it was not God who was accusing him and tempting him.

God asked Job a series of questions through which He began to reveal His character and nature to Job. This built Job's faith. God led him out of the depths of despair by focusing his attention on Him and away from his troubles.

God's questions caused Job to realize the magnificence of his Lord. The questions dealt with the wonders of creation. Who made the earth? Who made the boundaries of the oceans? Who made snow and hail? Who feeds lions and ravens? Who makes horses strong and eagles to nest on mountaintops? (See Job 38:4–39:30.)

God wanted Job to realize he was not to accuse Him of doing anything evil toward him, so He continued to ask question Job.

> *Now prepare yourself like a man; I will question you, and you shall answer Me: Would you indeed annul My judgment? Would you condemn Me that you may be justified?*
> (Job 40:7–8)

God pointed out a fatal flaw in Job's thinking. Again, Job thought his good deeds made him righteous before God. He thought he should not have to suffer because he had done good works. He failed to realize he could be justified by faith alone and not by works.

Job could not save himself. He had to accept the fact that he was not righteous because of his deeds, but that he was righteous only by faith in God. He then had to accept his righteousness in God by faith.

Jesus is the only One who was completely righteous. (See Hebrews 4:15.) Like Job, we cannot be made righteous by our own works. Yet, by recognizing our need for a Savior, we, too, can accept God's provision for righteousness. Our righteousness comes only by faith in Jesus Christ. (See Romans 3:21–22.)

God continued to reveal more about Himself to Job. He overwhelmed Job with His greatness. (See Job 40:9–41:34.) This progressive revelation brought Job to a point of greater faith and trust in Him. Job took his eyes off his terrible situation and focused instead on the wonders and glory of God. When Job shifted his attention from his problems to the wonders of the Creator, he realized his mistake. He saw God in a positive light and recognized that God was not the cause of his problems.

Job received faith through his conversation with God, from hearing His Word. God's Word and instruction took Job from a place of great fear to a place of faith. And his faith in God is what helped him to make the necessary changes in his life to have victory over his circumstances.

By Admitting He Was Wrong

Job's personal interaction with God broke the limitations in his life and brought him to a place of repentance. When he saw God's goodness and compared it with his own "goodness," he saw how inadequate he was. Here is what Job told God when he realized he had falsely blamed Him for his problems:

> *I know that You can do everything, and that no purpose of Yours can be withheld from You. You asked, "Who is this who hides counsel without knowledge?" Therefore I have uttered what I did not understand, things too wonderful for me, which I did not know. Listen, please, and let me speak; You said, "I will question you, and you shall answer Me." I have heard of You by the hearing of the ear, but now my eye sees You. Therefore I abhor myself, and repent in dust and ashes.* (Job 42:1–6)

Job now understood the goodness of God. He saw that he needed to put his trust completely in God's plan and purpose for his life.

Job then repented from his self-righteousness. He accepted the grace of God and was restored. His restoration was not just a spiritual restoration but also included his health, his prosperity, and his peace of mind.

JOB TRIUMPHED OVER THE POWER OF THE DEVIL

Job is a good example of a man who, with God's help, triumphed over his limits. Faith in God brought him salvation and deliverance from his circumstances and caused him to have victory over the power of the devil.

Job's triumph over his suffering came when he had a better understanding of the goodness and grace of God. He gained a deeper understanding of God's nature and developed an overcoming faith in His power to deliver and heal. Job gave the world a wonderful illustration of God's ability to alleviate and redeem the sufferings of humanity from poverty, disease, sorrow, and despair.

> JOB'S VICTORY OVER HIS SUFFERING CAME WHEN HE HAD A BETTER UNDERSTANDING OF THE GOODNESS AND GRACE OF GOD.

Now the LORD blessed the latter days of Job more than his beginning; for he had fourteen thousand sheep, six thousand camels, one thousand yoke of oxen, and one thousand female donkeys. He also had seven sons and three daughters. And he called the name of the first Jemimah, the name of the second Keziah, and the name of the third Keren-Happuch. In all the land were found no women so beautiful as the daughters of Job; and their father gave them an inheritance among their brothers. After this Job lived one hundred and forty years, and saw his children and grandchildren for four generations. So Job died, old and full of days.

(Job 42:12–17)

You Can Triumph Over Your Circumstances

The account of Job ends in a great triumph. God restored everything the devil had taken from him. He saved him from all his troubles. He caused him to triumph over sickness, poverty, sorrow, and despair. He restored his riches, his health, and his family. Job's story is an example of how God wants to bless His people.

Jesus came to destroy the works of the devil. He wants you to triumph over the limiting circumstances in your life. You, too, can have victory over sickness, poverty, sorrow, and despair. Jesus can make you triumphant over every attack of the devil.

You can hear the voice of God. You can read His precious promises in the Bible. You can have a victorious faith that overcomes the limitations of the world. No matter how terrible your circumstances, and no matter how severely you have been attacked by the devil, there are no hindrances that God cannot help you overcome. Faith and grace can enable you to triumph over all your circumstances, just as Job triumphed over his. There are no more limits that can stand against you!

Chapter Six

Conquering Tests and Hardships

As we saw in the life of Job, one of the enemy's tactics is to get you to blame God for all your problems. The devil makes people think God is working to destroy their lives, when, in reality, he is the one responsible for the destruction. The book of Job clearly shows that it was the devil who came to kill Job's children and servants. It was the devil who caused men to steal all his valuable livestock. It was the devil who afflicted his body with painful sores. The devil was working behind the scenes to bring ruin and destruction into Job's life.

Many Christians do not understand why things happen the way they do. Since they think everything that comes to pass in their lives is from God, they go from one bad circumstance to another without questioning these circumstances. They are blind to spiritual realities and are limited by their lack of knowledge. The god of this world, the devil, has deceived them, and many of them never recognize his deceitfulness. They go through life without perceiving the subtle (and sometimes not-so-subtle) limitations they have accepted in their lives. These limitations have their origin in darkness and are the result of the enemy's craftiness and lies.

THINGS DO NOT ALWAYS WORK OUT FOR GOOD

Some people try to find the good in all their circumstances. They have been taught that "all things work together for good," but they are not sure what that phrase means. It is a partial quotation from Romans 8:38, and they use it as a blanket statement to cover any problems they may face. This perspective is another example of a religious tradition that does more harm than good.

For instance, if a tree falls on the house of a person who has such a mind-set, he will say, "Well, you know, all things work together for good." If that person has a car wreck, he says, "All things work together for good." If his brother-in-law dies of cancer, he says, "All things work together for good."

People like this have been told that everything works together for good, even though they don't know how all these kinds of things work together for good. They fail to take into consideration that they have a spiritual enemy who is trying to ruin them spiritually, physically, mentally, and emotionally, and they are blind to his evil schemes at work in their lives.

All things do not always work out for the good. A person dying and going to hell is not good. A baby dying of malnutrition or starvation is not good. Wars that kill millions of people are not good. Drunk drivers injuring or killing other people is not good. Floods, hurricanes, and famines are not good. Sin, sickness, poverty, and disease are not good. These things have their origin in the devil.

What Does "All Things Work Together for Good" Mean?

If not everything that happens is good, what does "all things work together for good" really mean? To better understand this concept, let us look at Romans 8, where the quotation comes from:

> We know that all things work together for good to those who love God, to those who are the called according to His purpose.
>
> (Romans 8:28)

There is a lot more to this verse than "*all things work together for good.*" The rest of the verse gives us valuable insight into what this phrase refers to. It says, "*...to those who love God, to those who are the called according to His purpose.*"

This verse is telling us that all things work together for good when the proper conditions are met. The conditions are: you have to love God, and you have to be obedient to His calling for your life. If you are not in love with God, and if you are not being obedient to Him and serving Him according to His purpose for your life, you cannot say, "*All things work together for good.*"

It is vital that you understand God's will for your life. His Word will instruct you in His ways. God has a plan and a purpose for your life. He has predestined you to be conformed to the image of His Son Jesus.

Not all the circumstances you come across in life are God's will for you. You will have problems. You will face battles every day. There are spiritual forces at work behind the scenes that shape your circumstances. You live in a fallen world that is in darkness. The darkness causes suffering and hardships. Trials and tribulations are an inevitable part of life that you must learn to deal with.

YOUR FAITH IN GOD'S WORD WILL BE TRIED

> **THE WORD OF GOD IS LIKE SEED IN YOUR HEART; YOUR HEART IS A FIELD WHERE THE WORD IS SOWN.**

A major challenge you will face is the temptation to give up on God's Word. The Word of God is like seed in your heart; your heart is a field where the Word is sown. Some seeds never grow, and some seeds grow and produce a harvest. Jesus tells us that God's Word will be tested by adverse circumstances. His Word in your heart is what the devil will try to steal, because he wants to keep you from receiving your blessings from God.

> *The sower sows the word. And these are the ones by the wayside where the word is sown. When they hear, Satan comes immediately and takes away the word that was sown in their hearts.* (Mark 4:14–15)

The devil does not want God to be glorified through your faith in His Word. If you do not produce a harvest from God's Word, the devil will be able to "beat you up." You will have to settle for sickness, disease, and poverty. You will have to accept defeat. The devil wants you to become angry at God and to stop believing that His Word is true.

> *These likewise are the ones sown on stony ground who, when they hear the word, immediately receive it with gladness; and they have no root in themselves, and so endure only for a time. Afterward, when tribulation or persecution arises for the word's sake, immediately they stumble.* (Mark 4:16–17)

Recognize that your faith in God's Word will be tried. Trouble is sent to discourage you and to attempt to deceive you into believing that the Word is not working. The devil wants to destroy your faith in what God has said. You can fail at this point, or you can continue to believe that God's Word is true and receive your harvest.

You should also expect your faith to stand. Your faith is based on the completed work of Jesus Christ. Jesus strengthens you in your weakness and will always cause you to triumph over your tests and trials.

> *My brethren, count it all joy when you fall into various trials, knowing that the testing of your faith produces patience. But let patience have its perfect work, that you may be perfect and complete, lacking nothing.*
> (James 1:2–4)

You cannot escape problems and difficulties in life. You can, however, choose to be an overcomer and rise above your problems and difficulties.

SUFFERING FOR THE WRONG REASONS

In light of the above Scripture passage, I need to explain that there are two types of suffering. Many people misunderstand what it means to suffer for the Lord. You can suffer as a Christian for doing good, or you can suffer as a result of disobedience or ignorance; you can suffer as a result of not obeying God or believing that His Word is true. The second type of suffering is avoidable.

> *If you are reproached for the name of Christ, blessed are you, for the Spirit of glory and of God rests upon you. On their part He is blasphemed, but on your part He is glorified. But let none of you suffer as a murderer, a thief, an evildoer, or as a busybody in other people's matters. Yet if anyone suffers as a Christian, let him not be ashamed, but let him glorify God in this matter.*
> (1 Peter 4:14–16)

In chapter 3, we talked about the how the Israelites who left Egypt could not enter the Promised Land because they disobeyed God. Their children entered in, but they could not enter in because of their unbelief. They lost the right to live in the Promised Land because of fear, doubt, and rebellion against God. They would not have had to suffer by living in the wilderness if they had been obedient to Him.

SUFFERING FOR THE RIGHT REASONS

The apostle Paul had to endure many hardships. For example, he suffered many relentless attacks from a messenger of Satan; this evil force violently harassed him on his journeys. He was also shipwrecked. He experienced fierce opposition to his ministry by angry Jews. At various times, he was beaten, he was whipped, and he was stoned and left for dead. He suffered for doing good. (See 2 Corinthians 11:23–29; Acts 14:19–20.) However, Paul was able to say with confidence that the Lord delivered him from all his hardships.

> *Persecutions, afflictions, which happened to me at Antioch, at Iconium, at Lystra; what persecutions I endured. And out of them all the Lord delivered me.*　　(2 Timothy 3:11)

Paul even boasted about his own weaknesses, believing that the Lord's strength would carry him through them. He realized he had been made more than a conqueror through Christ who loved him.

The apostle Paul suffered for the Lord. He was persecuted for his faith. To suffer for the Lord is a trial of your faith. Temptations and hardships come to test you, but with faith and patience, you can overcome all of them.

DO NOT SUFFER NEEDLESSLY

Do not suffer needlessly by misunderstanding the difference between suffering for righteousness and suffering for foolishness. Again, an example of noble suffering is undergoing persecution after you have done something good. Needless suffering is experiencing anguish after you have disobeyed God and sinned.

SUFFERING BECAUSE YOU MISUNDERSTAND THE GOODNESS OF GOD, OR BECAUSE YOU CONTINUE TO SIN, IS SUFFERING FOR THE WRONG REASON.

Suffering for your faith, as the apostles and other martyrs did, is an honorable type of suffering. Suffering because you misunderstand the goodness of God, or because you continue to sin, is suffering for the wrong reason.

As I said earlier, the devil will come and tempt you with evil. He will try to stop your faith from working. He wants to entangle you in sin. Sin creates problems and limitations in your life that are avoidable. Suffering for the wrong reasons causes needless pain and hardship on you and others.

> *For what credit is it if, when you are beaten for your faults, you take it patiently? But when you do good and suffer, if you take it patiently, this is commendable before God.*
> (1 Peter 2:20)

If you have made mistakes and sinned, God has made a way for you to purify yourself and receive forgiveness.

> *If we confess our sins, He is faithful and just to forgive us our sins and to cleanse us from all unrighteousness.* (1 John 1:9)

Asking God to forgive you and then forsaking your sins settles the issue. It puts you back in right standing with God, so that you are blameless in His sight. He sees you through the righteousness of His

Son Jesus. You have the right to come boldly into God's presence to find the help you need. (See Hebrews 4:14–16.)

I believe that most Christians today suffer for the wrong reasons. They suffer not because they are being persecuted for being good but because they are doing things they should not do. Or, they suffer as a result of spiritual blindness, which keeps people from knowing or believing the promises of God. Lack of knowledge about the rights, privileges, and blessings available to you through Jesus can open the door for the devil to destroy you.

> *My people are destroyed for lack of knowledge. Because you have rejected knowledge, I also will reject you from being priest for Me; because you have forgotten the law of your God.* (Hosea 4:6)

God does not promise you a life free from problems. He does not guarantee that you will not suffer. However, He does not want you to suffer for the wrong reasons, either. Suffering for the wrong reasons is a problem that imposes limitations on you. If you are going to experience the blessing of no more limits in your life, you have to learn to discern God's will in regard to suffering and hardships. You should avoid needless suffering.

Conquering Tests and Hardships Through Jesus

Recognize That Jesus Overcame the Devil

Jesus came into the world to be a blessing to those around Him. He wanted people to enjoy the good gifts of a loving Father. He also came into the world to battle the darkness. Though He was tempted by the devil, He overcame the limits of the devil's tests and hardships and earned the right to be called "more than a conqueror." (See Romans 8:37.)

The apostle Peter said that our adversary, the devil, roams around like a lion, seeking to devour us, and that we should resist him. (See 1 Peter 5:8–9.) He also said,

> *The Lord knows how to deliver the godly out of temptations and to reserve the unjust under punishment for the day of judgment.*
> (2 Peter 2:9)

Temptations are tests and hardships. Since Jesus experienced and overcame all the limits of the devil and the world, you can overcome all your temptations through Him.

You are not the only one who has ever had to experience tests and hardships. Everyone experiences these things. Paul wrote,

> *No temptation has overtaken you except such as is common to man; but God is faithful, who will not allow you to be tempted beyond what you are able, but with the temptation will also make the way of escape, that you may be able to bear it.*
> (1 Corinthians 10:13)

We must come to truly understand that we do not have to defeat the devil, because Jesus has

already defeated him. However-
er, the devil has not yet been
removed from the earth. His
work, and his followers, are
still active in the world today.
There are spiritual battles
taking place around us all
the time. We still have to fight
the good fight of faith, but we
can always be triumphant
because of Jesus.

> WE STILL HAVE
> TO FIGHT THE
> GOOD FIGHT OF
> FAITH, BUT WE
> CAN ALWAYS BE
> TRIUMPHANT
> BECAUSE OF JESUS.

PUT ON THE ARMOR OF GOD

In his letter to the Ephesians, Paul used the illustration of a battle-ready soldier to describe what
we experience in life. He said to put on the armor of
God to be able to withstand all the evil in the world.
(See Ephesians 6:10–18.) Paul acknowledged the existence of evil powers. Because he knew his enemies,
he wrote,

> *For we do not wrestle against flesh and
> blood, but against principalities, against
> powers, against the rulers of the darkness
> of this age, against spiritual hosts of wick-
> edness in the heavenly places.*
>
> (Ephesians 6:12)

Paul knew believers would be involved in spiritual battles. You are to wear the armor of God to stand
against, and be victorious over, all the tactics and
attacks of your spiritual enemy. You can withstand
these attacks by being strong in the power of God.

Operate in Jesus' Authority

Remember that Jesus came to destroy the works of the devil. Sickness, poverty, and crime are tests and hardships caused by Satan.

> *He who sins is of the devil, for the devil has sinned from the beginning. For this purpose the Son of God was manifested, that He might destroy the works of the devil.*
> (1 John 3:8)

Jesus came to give you power to overcome all the power of the enemy. That includes all oppression, disease, and death.

> *Then the seventy* [disciples] *returned with joy, saying, "Lord, even the demons are subject to us in Your name." And He said to them, "I saw Satan fall like lightning from heaven. Behold, I give you the authority to trample on serpents and scorpions, and over all the power of the enemy, and nothing shall by any means hurt you."*
> (Luke 10:17–19)

You have authority in the name of Jesus to overcome the enemy and the limitations he tries to bring into your life and the lives of others.

Submit to God and Resist the Devil

The apostle James also described how to win spiritual battles. He offered some practical advice for believers when he wrote,

Therefore submit to God. Resist the devil and he will flee from you. (James 4:7)

James's advice is simple. Submit yourself to God and resist the devil, and the enemy will leave you alone. Resisting the devil is important. You must learn how to resist him and fight against him. You must stand firm against his attempts to steal, kill, and destroy.

YOU ARE MORE THAN A CONQUEROR OVER TESTS AND HARDSHIPS

The words of the apostle Paul and the apostle James do not sound like the words of men who were used to being defeated by the devil. Their words sound like those of experienced followers of Jesus telling us how we can overcome the devil's attacks.

Tests and hardships come to limit your life, but God has the solution for every test and hardship known to humanity, and He has the answer to all the problems you will ever experience. Your answers are found in the victory and triumph of Jesus Christ over all the limitations the devil would try to impose on you. Jesus allows you to walk in His victory and to appropriate all His resources.

> JESUS ALLOWS YOU TO WALK IN HIS VICTORY AND TO APPROPRIATE ALL HIS RESOURCES.

The apostle Paul emphatically stated that through all the tests and hardships of life, Jesus is always ready to help you. He said you are not a helpless sheep being led to slaughter. You are more than a conqueror through Jesus who loved you and made you an overcomer.

> *Who shall separate us from the love of Christ? Shall tribulation, or distress, or persecution, or famine, or nakedness, or peril, or sword? As it is written: "For Your sake we are killed all day long; we are accounted as sheep for the slaughter." Yet in all these things we are more than conquerors through Him who loved us.* (Romans 8:35–37)

Chapter Seven

The Unlimited Power Within You

As a Christian, you have been given spiritual power to live life victoriously. This type of power cannot be seen with the natural eyes, though others can see its effects in you and around you. The Holy Spirit is the power that lives within all Christians. As God, He is all-powerful, and He wants to express Himself through you.

Some people are carriers of dormant viruses. These viruses could be activated at any time and bring death and misery. Most people would believe a doctor if he or she told them they had a deadly virus inside them. However, when a preacher tells them the power of God is inside them, they do not believe it. This should not be. We should believe God's Word. What is within us is much more powerful than we can imagine. It is the same power that is available to help us proclaim the good news of Jesus to a dying world.

But you shall receive power when the Holy Spirit has come upon you; and you shall be witnesses to Me in Jerusalem, and in all

> *Judea and Samaria, and to the end of the
> earth.*   (Acts 1:8)

The power of God inside you strengthens your body and helps you to overcome the effects of your human weaknesses:

> *For though* [Jesus] *was crucified in weakness, yet He lives by the power of God. For we also are weak in Him, but we shall live with Him by the power of God toward you.*
> (2 Corinthians 13:4)

The power of God inside you enables you to receive from Him whatever you need. This power makes it possible for God to say He can do more than we could ever ask or imagine.

> *Now to Him who is able to do exceedingly abundantly above all that we ask or think, according to the power that works in us.*
> (Ephesians 3:20)

The same Holy Spirit who was active in creating the universe is within you. (See Genesis 1:1–2.) Therefore, the power of God inside you is full of life. You have an unlimited resource available to you that allows you to enter into the realm of "no more limits." The Spirit will help you learn and understand God's will. He will help you live a life that glorifies God. The more you understand how the Holy Spirit's power is made available to you through Jesus, the more you will be able to tap into it for your needs and the needs of others.

KNOWLEDGE ACTIVATES THE POWER OF GOD

Your body has a natural defense mechanism, known as your immune system. There are germs all around you. If you did not have a good immune system, you would quickly die. Germs may enter your body, but because your immune system protects you, you may never even know it. If you have a strong immune system, it attacks germs that enter your body before they can harm you.

Similarly, the power of God within you helps you to fend off harmful spiritual attacks against you. Spend time learning about the person of the Holy Spirit and how He wants to move in your life. Studying the Word of God will help you to better know the nature of the power within you, and knowledge of God's will for your life will enable you to activate this power.

> Grace and peace be multiplied to you in the knowledge of God and of Jesus our Lord, as His divine power has given to us all things that pertain to life and godliness, through the knowledge of Him who called us by glory and virtue. (2 Peter 1:2–3)

Note that God's power has been given to those whom He has called "by glory and virtue." Your calling is important. When you are fulfilling God's call on your life, you will see the results of the power of God. You will find yourself receiving all the things you need for your life and for carrying out your call.

Peter used the past tense in this verse when he said that God "has given to us all things that pertain *to life and godliness."* The phrase *"has given"* means it is already done. This power is already available and ready to assist you. Every single thing you need for life can be obtained by the power that works in you.

You must build a spiritual immune system that helps you in time of need, because you must come to the place where you automatically resist spiritual forces that oppose you. When your mind has been renewed by the Word of God, you can tell which things in your life are from God and which things are not. (See Romans 12:2.) If you do not know God and His ways, you will not be able to fight against the things that are contrary to His will. But if you do know God and His ways, your spiritual immune system will have the power to protect you.

> IF YOU KNOW GOD AND HIS WAYS, YOUR SPIRITUAL IMMUNE SYSTEM WILL HAVE THE POWER TO PROTECT YOU.

God's power is working in you to accomplish His purpose for your life. Again, to receive the fulfillment of this promise, you have to know God. You must study and gain knowledge of Him, and you must apply His Word to your life. You also need to guard your heart to keep yourself from missing His will.

> *My son, give attention to my words; incline your ear to my sayings. Do not let them depart from your eyes; keep them in the midst of your heart; for they are life to those who find them, and health to all their flesh. Keep your heart with all diligence, for out of it spring the issues of life.* (Proverbs 4:20–23)

The Bible is like a will that designates you as Jesus' beneficiary. Imagine if you were to wake up one day and discover that a long-lost relative had left you a large sum of money in his will. The Bible is much more than a will from a rich relative. It is a will from the Ruler of the universe!

God has promised you *everything* that pertains to life and godliness. The Bible is His will for your life. It tells you what legally belongs to you in the kingdom of God. It also tells you how to receive what is rightfully yours. In addition, the Bible is a road map for living. It is a guide to help you know how to walk as His child. God activates His Word by the power of His Spirit within you.

YOU PARTAKE OF GOD'S NATURE THROUGH HIS PROMISES

The apostle Peter wrote,

> [God's] *divine power has given to us all things that pertain to life and godliness, through the knowledge of Him who called us by glory and virtue, by which have been given to us exceedingly great and precious promises, that through these you may be partakers of the divine nature, having escaped the corruption that is in the world through lust.* (2 Peter 1:3–4)

God has given you promises so that you might receive a new life and a new nature. You may partake of His divine nature—this is a tremendous promise! However, some people misunderstand this concept. The Scripture does not say you will *be* God;

it says you will be *like* Him. In other words, you will have the ability to reflect His nature and ways. Every Christian has precious promises that allow him or her to be conformed to the image of Jesus Christ. (See Romans 8:29.) These promises allow you to escape the evil in the world.

In the above passage, we find the word *"exceedingly"* again. God has given you unlimited promises. He has given you these promises so you can have His character and power in your life. You can use the promises God has given you to glorify Him.

You Partake of God's Promises by Being Fully Persuaded

God says you can be a partaker of His divine nature, but the way you partake of this nature is by being convinced of the precious promises found in His Word, so that you act on them in faith. God gave Abraham precious promises that he would be blessed and become a blessing to the whole world. He told Abraham he would have a child by his wife, Sarah. This would be a miracle because Abraham was one hundred years old and Sarah was ninety years old and well past the age of being able to conceive a child. (See Genesis 17:17.) Yet Abraham did not waver regarding the promises of God. (See Romans 4:20.) He had great faith. The apostle Paul mentioned Abraham's faith, saying that he was *"fully convinced that what* [God] *had promised He was also able to perform"* (Romans 4:21).

Paul was describing how Abraham was *"fully convinced"* God was going to bless him with a child through Sarah. God had given him a promise, and he took God at His word. Sarah did have a child, and

Abraham became the *"father of many nations"* (Genesis 17:4, 5). And, again, one of Abraham's descendants was Jesus Christ.

When you believe God's promises are true, even when the circumstances look bad, you are demonstrating faith in Him. Abraham was fully convinced that God's promises were true. You, too, can be fully convinced that God's promises are true, and you can be blessed.

Here, then, is the key to partaking of God's divine nature. God has given you promises. God also has given you the power to believe His promises. His promises are activated when you are fully convinced that He is able to do what He has said He will do. When you have faith in God's promises, the power of the Holy Spirit works in you and through you to bring them to pass. This is the way to enter into a life where God is able to do exceedingly abundantly above all you can ask or imagine.

When you read and act on the promises of God, which are His will for your life, you can be completely convinced that He can fulfill His promises. The more you meditate on the promises found in the Bible, the more you will be persuaded that God is able and willing to bring them to pass.

THE MORE YOU MEDITATE ON THE PROMISES FOUND IN THE BIBLE, THE MORE YOU WILL BE PERSUADED THAT GOD IS ABLE AND WILLING TO BRING THEM TO PASS.

We have read in 2 Peter 1:4 that the promises will help you escape the corruption and lust in the world. If you are fully convinced, you will not act on the temptation to be drawn away into unbelief. If you are fully persuaded, you will not act on thoughts of worry, fear, or failure. The Holy Spirit, the power of God working in you, will keep you from falling into the traps of the enemy. (See Jude 24.)

A LIFE THAT EXPRESSES GOD'S POWER BRINGS GLORY TO HIM

I mentioned in chapter 1 that God has a predetermined plan for your life. He has called you, justified you, and glorified you. (See Romans 8:30.) And earlier in this chapter, we saw that He has called you *"by glory and virtue"* (2 Peter 1:3). What does it mean to be called by glory and virtue?

By this phrase, Peter was saying that God put His glory in you when you became a Christian. The Holy Spirit within you is a gift from God to help you lead a life of virtue that gives glory to Him. (See John 16:5–15.) When we do things that bring glory to God, we are fulfilling His plan for our lives. Doing good works and living triumphantly through Jesus Christ are acts that bring glory to the Father. Living a life that expresses His power brings glory to Him.

Before you became a Christian, you were spiritually broken and helpless. Then, Christ removed your sins and gave you a new spiritual life, and God established you spiritually to be able to receive His power. He put His glory and power within you, so you have all you need to be successful in this life. God wants you to experience His abundant life. You therefore need to activate the power of the Holy Spirit within you. To summarize, you activate His power by first gaining knowledge about God, and then by operating in faith according to what you know.

OVERCOMING LIMITATIONS ON THE POWER OF GOD

There are times when the power of God is limited in believers' lives. This entire book is written for the purpose of helping you remove the limits that are keeping you from experiencing the life God has for you.

In chapter 3, we defined limitations as boundaries that keep us separated from the resources of heaven, and we discussed what some of those boundaries are, such as provoking, grieving, and tempting God. Let us now discuss three additional limitations that hinder the power of God in our lives, which have to do with our attitudes. These three limitations are (1) feelings of unworthiness, (2) false humility, and (3) being easily offended.

When we change our attitudes and renew our minds according to the Word of God, we become free to receive what God has planned for us and to operate in the unlimited power of the Holy Spirit within us.

1. FEELINGS OF UNWORTHINESS

An attitude of unworthiness can be a product of guilt, condemnation, or failure. It can also be a product of wrong doctrine. Some Christians teach that believers are unworthy, that they are like "old worms in the dust" or "mud pots for Jesus"; just undeserving pilgrims trudging through life in the heat and the cold. Yes, God has saved us, these Christians say, but we are still sorry, no-good messes.

If you hear this "unworthy" message from a pastor long enough, you will leave every church service feeling lower than you came. After years and years of this type of wrong teaching, you will develop wrong thinking, imagining that you are not really valuable to God or anyone else, and that God does not care about you. You will put limits on yourself.

These limits will keep you from believing you are worthy to receive anything from God. You will not think He wants to do anything for you. You might think He loves your pastor or some famous preacher, but you are not sure He loves you.

In a significant sense, all people have the same background: we were all sinners. We were all unworthy to receive the blessings of God. Not one of us was righteous by ourselves before God. Fortunately for all of us, Jesus came and died in our place. God loved us so much that He sent Jesus to pay the price for our sins. When we accepted Jesus Christ as Lord of our lives, He put new life within us. This life has eternal value, because it is born of God.

When God gave you eternal life, He took away the old life and replaced it with something new. Your new life is based on what Jesus has done for you. You were unworthy to approach God on your own behalf, but Jesus prepared a way for you to be brought into the presence of God on His merits.

> JESUS IS THE DOOR FOR YOU TO ENTER INTO THE BLESSINGS OF GOD.

You became like Jesus when you accepted Him as your Lord, and Jesus is the door for you to enter into the blessings of God. You are now worthy to be used for His glory.

To say you are not worthy to be used by God is to ig-nore who you are—right now—in Christ. You are no longer a sinner saved by grace. You *were* a sinner, you *were* saved by grace, and you have now *become* the righteousness of God in Christ.

> [God] *made* [Jesus] *who knew no sin to be sin for us, that we might become the righ-teousness of God in Him.*
> (2 Corinthians 5:21)

You can do nothing in yourself, but, through Je-sus Christ, you have been made the righteousness of God. God has sent the Holy Spirit to live in you and to give you the power to do His will. You were bought with a price, so you should not live selfishly, but you should glorify God in all your actions.

> *Do you not know that your body is the tem-ple of the Holy Spirit who is in you, whom you have from God, and you are not your own? For you were bought at a price; there-fore glorify God in your body and in your spirit, which are God's.*
> (1 Corinthians 6:19–20)

You are valuable and precious to God. You are worth something because He paid for your redemp-tion from sin with the blood of His only Son Jesus. You have been made worthy to be blessed by God, and you have been made worthy to be a blessing to others. Your value outside of Jesus is nothing, but your value in Jesus is priceless.

Unfortunately, there will always be Christians who are limited by the religious tradition that says

they are "unworthy." Under this tradition, "unworthiness" is a badge of honor, so these people fail to
see the reality of what Jesus has made them. They
are not unworthy if they have been born again. If the
Holy Spirit has given them life, they have been made
worthy by the death and resurrection of Jesus.

When you start saying you are worthy to be
blessed, the "unworthy" religious people may dis-
agree with you and accuse you of being arrogant.
It is not arrogant to accept the gift of grace God has
given you. You are not worthy because you have done
anything yourself; you are worthy because of what
Jesus has done. He has made you worthy, and all the
glory goes to God.

When you understand that you are valuable
because of Jesus, you are on your way to removing
the limitation of feelings of unworthiness. Removing
this limitation will help you to receive all God has
planned for you.

2. False Humility

An attitude of false humility will also limit you
in life. It is different from an attitude of unworthiness. Unworthiness is a result of bad doctrines, poor
upbringing, or struggles with life's difficulties, but
false humility is a form of pride. Pride will keep you
from being blessed by God. False humility is trying
to be something you are not. For instance, you do not
believe you are humble, but you are *acting* humble to
impress others. False humility is phony. If you have
this attitude, you need to eliminate it so you can be
who God wants you to be and do what God wants
you to do.

Likewise you younger people, submit your-selves to your elders. Yes, all of you be sub-missive to one another, and be clothed with humility, for "God resists the proud, but gives grace to the humble." (1 Peter 5:5)

False humility is a stench in the nostrils of God. He will not bless pride and arrogance. Let go of false humility and walk in true humility, and God will exalt you in His time.

Therefore humble yourselves under the mighty hand of God, that He may exalt you in due time. (verse 6)

Real humility is an honorable attribute. It is acting on who you are in Christ. You realize that you can do nothing in your own strength, that it is only through the power of God within you that you will become and accomplish what He

> REAL HUMILITY IS ACTING ON WHO YOU ARE IN CHRIST.

has planned. True humility is a beautiful thing and demonstrates that you know your place before God. Your place before God is based on who you are in Christ and not on who you are in yourself.

3. BEING EASILY OFFENDED

Many people limit God because they take offense easily. Being offended is the result of a wrong attitude toward God, Jesus, or someone else. Offenses are traps placed by the enemy to limit the power of God from operating in your life. I believe most people today could not handle the words of Jesus if they were to hear Him speak in person. If He pastored a church, He would probably drive away many of the members of His congregation. He would speak the truth in love, but most people would be offended by His truthfulness.

I often say things in love to people to try to help them, and it sometimes upsets them. I try to say things as lovingly as I know how, but there are just certain people who have an "offense meter" that is very sensitive. Some people will run away from the truth because they love the darkness more than the light. (See John 3:19–21.)

Walking in love means forgiving people. Forgiveness is a powerful force that takes limits off God so He can work in your life.

> *And whenever you stand praying, if you have anything against anyone, forgive him, that your Father in heaven may also forgive you your trespasses. But if you do not forgive, neither will your Father in heaven forgive your trespasses.*   (Mark 11:25–26)

Letting go of offenses and walking in the truth and love of God will allow you to experience more of the unlimited power of God within you.

WHAT YOU DO AFFECTS HOW PEOPLE VIEW GOD

Whether you want to believe it or not, when people are looking at you as a Christian, they form an opinion about God. God has called you to be His representative; you are an ambassador for Christ.

Now then, we are ambassadors for Christ,
as though God were pleading through us:
we implore you on Christ's behalf, be recon-
ciled to God.   (2 Corinthians 5:20)

I understand this is a sensitive area in some
people's lives, but I must say it again: How you live
your life as a Christian gives other people an impression about God.

If you limit God from working in your life, you
will cause others to have a limited perspective of
Him. If you communicate attitudes of unworthiness
or false humility, you will give people the wrong idea
about the freedom and blessing they can find in Him.
If you are easily offended and have unforgiveness in
your heart, you will portray these things to others,
and they will fail to see God's forgiveness through
Christ. When you exhibit wrong attitudes and be-
haviors, you limit God in the eyes of others by not
revealing His true character.

When people see you, what do they learn about
God? Do you represent Him well?

Some people look at the way many Christians
live and want to have nothing to do with God. When
they see you poor, they think that God is poor. When
they see you prospering, they think that God is prospering. Right or wrong, these things influence people. When you are blessed in all areas of your life,
when you are walking in health, and when you are
prospering financially, you are a positive example to
others of the life God wants for us.

Please be careful with this, however. You should
not want to be blessed for the purpose of keeping up
with what other people are doing. For example, you

might come to love money, get greedy, and damage your relationship with God. You should want to be blessed by God for the right reasons—to glorify Him and to be able to help others. God wants you to be blessed, but your priorities need to be right.

> *But seek first the kingdom of God and His righteousness, and all these things shall be added to you.* (Matthew 6:33)

WHEN YOUR PRIORITIES ARE IN THE PROPER ORDER, YOU CAN BE BLESSED IN ALL AREAS OF YOUR LIFE.

When your priorities are in the proper order, you can be blessed in all areas of your life. And when you are obeying God and serving Him with good intentions, you will be able to be an example for others to follow. This does not mean that you will never have problems or suffer persecution or afflictions. It means that you will have the power working within you that allows you to bring glory to God through all your circumstances.

> *Fear not, little flock; for it is your Father's good pleasure to give you the kingdom.* (Luke 12:32)

God takes great pleasure in blessing you. If you could just understand how God is more than willing to do *"exceedingly abundantly"* above all you could ask or think, your limits would be shattered.

> *Now to Him who is able to do exceedingly abundantly above all that we ask or think,*

according to the power that works in us, to Him be glory in the church by Christ Jesus to all generations, forever and ever. Amen.
(Ephesians 3:20–21)

God makes all this possible by the power He has given you through the Holy Spirit, who lives in you. You are the temple of the Holy Spirit. You are the "container" of God's power. When you lay hands on the sick, He is laying hands on the sick. When you feed the hungry and clothe the naked, He is doing these acts through you. He wants you to remove your limits so He can use you to bring glory to Himself through your life and actions. He will do so through the unlimited power of the Holy Spirit within you.

Chapter Eight

Receiving God's Exceedingly Great Promises

Christians are often limited in their prayer lives because they do not understand how willing God is to meet their needs. Most believers are confident of God's ability to do anything, but many are not sure He is willing to do it for them today. We need to connect God's willingness with His ability.

One of the stories in the Bible that is most precious to me, and which illustrates God's willingness to meet our needs, is that of the man who came to Jesus to seek cleansing from the disease of leprosy. I have ministered in two leper colonies, and I have sensed the cries in those people's hearts and have seen the agony in their bodies. Lepers are often missing fingers, ears, and noses, which have been eaten away by the disease. The lepers' appearance makes them repulsive to most people, and they are social outcasts. It would be offensive to most people to consider touching a person with leprosy.

The disease of leprosy has been around for thousands of years. In ancient Israel, lepers were considered unclean and were forced to live away from most people. Whenever a leper went out in public, he or she had to cry out in a loud voice, "Unclean! Unclean!" Lepers were not allowed to associate with anyone except other lepers. So, it was only out of desperation that a leper approached Jesus one day. We can still hear his desperate plea for help from the story of his encounter with Jesus in the book of Mark.

> *Now a leper came to Him, imploring Him, kneeling down to Him and saying to Him, "If You are willing, You can make me clean."*
> (Mark 1:40)

The leper had heard of the marvelous things Jesus had done for other people. He had heard of Jesus' miraculous abilities and how He had healed many others, and He knew Jesus was able to heal him. However, he was not sure if Jesus was *willing* to heal a man like him.

This leper represents all of us. We were all unclean and unworthy to approach God on our own merits. Paul wrote in Romans 3:23, *"All have sinned and fall short of the glory of God."* We need a Savior to cleanse us from our sins and to make us new. We know Jesus can cleanse our hearts, but do we know He is willing to help us with other needs in our lives?

Let us look at how Jesus responded to this man's plea for help.

> *Then Jesus, moved with compassion, stretched out His hand and touched him, and said to him, "I am willing; be cleansed."*
> (Mark 1:41)

Jesus demonstrated He was not only able but also willing to heal. Reaching out in love, He touched this man whom no one else was willing to touch, told him, *"I am willing; be cleansed,"* and healed him of his leprosy.

Jesus is also willing to help you. Whatever you are asking for, if it will glorify God, Jesus is able and willing to give it to you. He is willing to help you with anything you need. It does not have to be physical healing. It can be emotional healing; it can be a need for love. Jesus assured us,

> WHATEVER YOU ARE ASKING FOR, IF IT WILL GLORIFY GOD, JESUS IS ABLE AND WILLING TO GIVE IT TO YOU.

And whatever you ask in My name, that I will do, that the Father may be glorified in the Son. (John 14:13)

God wants to answer your prayers so He may be glorified through Jesus. He is able *and* willing to answer your prayers.

ASK GOD FOR ANYTHING ACCORDING TO HIS WILL

God will grant you whatever you ask. However, there is one important condition: He will answer your prayer only when you ask for something that is in accordance with His will.

Now this is the confidence that we have in Him, that if we ask anything according to

> *His will, He hears us. And if we know that*
> *He hears us, whatever we ask, we know*
> *that we have the petitions that we have*
> *asked of Him.*   (1 John 5:14–15)

Notice the words "*whatever we ask*." "*Whatever*" means "anything." There are no limits to what you can ask for when you are asking according to what God has willed for you.

WHAT IS THE WILL OF THE LORD?

I have heard some people add the expression "if it is Your will, Lord" to the ends of all their prayers. People are not really sure what the will of God is, so they use this blanket statement to cover themselves if their prayers are not answered. When you add this phrase to the end of a prayer, you are saying you are not sure what the will of God is in the situation.

Jesus prayed for God's will to be done and not His own. The cup He spoke of in the following verse is symbolic of His suffering and death.

> *Father, if it is Your will, take this cup away*
> *from Me; nevertheless not My will, but*
> *Yours, be done.*   (Luke 22:42)

Jesus prayed this prayer in the agony of the garden of Gethsemane, and He accepted that it was God's will for Him to die on the cross. There was no other way to redeem humanity from sin, sickness, poverty, and death except by His suffering and dying for the sins of the world—for your sins and mine. His death and resurrection made it possible for us to be overcomers and to receive abundant life.

A sinner never has to pray, "If it is Your will, Lord, save me." It is God's will to save sinners.

For "whoever calls on the name of the LORD shall be saved." (Romans 10:13)

Any person who is willing to change his or her life, and who asks God for salvation, will be saved. A simple prayer of faith, such as "God, save me!" is all that is necessary.

The initial prayer of salvation opens the door to more than a ticket to heaven. Salvation...

- allows Jesus to come and live within our hearts.
- brings a change in our lifestyles.
- entitles us to restoration, wholeness, and eternal life.

The traditions of men limit God by promoting prayers like "Lord, heal me, if it is Your will," or "Lord, meet my daily financial needs, if it is Your will." If it is clearly God's will in the Bible, it is clearly God's will for your life. Do not let tradition rob you of knowing God's will for you. Read your Bible prayerfully, and you will know His will for you concerning healing and having your needs met.

IS GOD'S WILL ALWAYS DONE?

God's will is not always done. Again, it is not God's will for any person to go to hell after death.

The Lord is not slack concerning His promise, as some count slackness, but is

longsuffering toward us, not willing that
any should perish but that all should come
to repentance. (2 Peter 3:9)

Do people go to hell? Yes, they go to hell against God's will every day. Jesus said that the road to hell is broad, and the road to life is narrow. (See Matthew 7:13–14.) Multitudes of people are on the broad road to hell against God's plan for their lives.

People use their own free will to reject the will of God. You can choose not to accept His will for your life, and He will honor your wishes. Simply because it is God's will for a person to be saved or blessed in an area does not mean that His will is being done. We have to recognize and receive God's will by faith.

> WE HAVE TO RECOGNIZE AND RECEIVE GOD'S WILL BY FAITH.

When people die and go to hell against the will of God, this does not change His will. The Lord will save whoever calls on His name. (See Romans 10:13.) Someone who dies of cancer does not change the will of God concerning healing. The fact that we were healed by Jesus' stripes is still true. (See 1 Peter 2:24.) Someone who goes bankrupt does not change the will of God. The fact that God will supply all our needs according to His riches in glory through Christ Jesus is still true. (See Philippians 4:19.) Someone who commits adultery or steals does not change the will of God. The fact that God has given us everything we need for life and godliness is still true. (See 2 Peter 1:3.) God does not endorse sin. People sin against His will all the time. Yet the sinful actions or inactions of others do not change the will of God for your life.

You have been given a free will to choose what you believe and what you do not believe. You should choose to serve and obey God. Joshua chose to serve and follow Him, as he declared in a speech to the Israelites:

> *And if it seems evil to you to serve the LORD, choose for yourselves this day whom you will serve, whether the gods which your fathers served that were on the other side of the River, or the gods of the Amorites, in whose land you dwell. But as for me and my house, we will serve the LORD.*
>
> (Joshua 24:15)

You and those in your household should choose to receive and obey the will of God. Obedience to God will result in the fulfillment of all His promises concerning your life. When you obey God and are serving Him according to His will, all things will work together for your good. (See Romans 8:28.)

MANY TRADITIONS NULLIFY THE WILL OF THE LORD

As we have seen, certain religious traditions declare that many things God did in the Bible are no longer His will. You know you are in trouble when religious leaders go to great lengths to explain why the Bible does not mean what it says. Religious traditions can nullify what the Scriptures teach. (See Matthew 15:3–8.)

Many of these religious traditions admit that the Bible is true, but then they render the Word of God ineffective in people's lives by saying it is not true for today. Again, they may say, "It is no longer God's will to heal today," and "Miracles have ceased." Some traditions admit God wants to bless you spiritually, but they stop short of saying God can help you pay your rent or fix your car. They say you cannot be certain if God is willing to help you with anything that is not spiritual, declaring, "You can never be sure of the will of the Lord."

Traditions therefore set limits on what people expect God to do for them. Some people have asked God for things but have not received them. Out of their experiences, they develop doctrines. Because they did not receive exactly what they prayed for, they assumed their request must not have been God's will. For example, someone may say, "I asked God for a new washing machine but got a scrub board, instead. It must be that God didn't want me to have that expensive washing machine." They put their experience above the Word of God and come to the wrong conclusion.

Let's look at another example in the area of healing. A person may say, "I prayed for my aunt to be healed from cancer, but she died." The person may conclude from this experience, "It must not be God's will to heal today." Many people look to the circumstances to determine the will of God. Yet the Word of God is a higher authority than circumstances. God's Word is true in spite of many traditions that say healing is no longer for today. (See Romans 3:3–4.)

You have a choice to base your faith on what has happened to others or on the promises of God. The Bible is full of promises. You will not be disappointed basing your faith on the Bible. You will be disappointed basing your faith on what happened to So-and-So.

Jesus came to earth and triumphed over sin, sickness, poverty, and all the power of the devil. It is not the will of God for any of His children to be subjected to a life under the power of the devil. God's will for your life is that you be victorious over *all* the power of the enemy. His will is that you *"reign in life"* (Romans 5:17) over your circumstances.

> GOD'S WILL FOR YOUR LIFE IS THAT YOU BE VICTORIOUS OVER *ALL* THE POWER OF THE ENEMY.

YOUR WILL BE DONE ON EARTH AS IT IS IN HEAVEN

The will of God is clear when you use the Bible as your guide. Jesus instructed His disciples to pray that God's will be done on earth as it is in heaven.

> *In this manner, therefore, pray: Our Father in heaven, hallowed be Your name. Your kingdom come. Your will be done on earth as it is in heaven. Give us this day our daily bread.* (Matthew 6:9–11)

This passage is part of what we call the Lord's Prayer. It really should be called the "Disciple's Prayer," because Jesus taught it to His disciples to help guide them in their prayer lives.

Think for a minute about the statement *"Your will be done on earth as it is in heaven."* Jesus taught that we should pray for God's will to be done on earth as it is done in heaven. When you read the Bible and note how wonderful things are in heaven, this gives you some idea of what God's will might be for you.

Is there sickness and disease in heaven? Of course not. Everything is healthy in heaven. Is there poverty in heaven? Of course not. The streets are paved with gold. Are there heartbreaks and disappointments in heaven? No, there is happiness and joy. If God's total will were to be done on earth as it is in heaven, there would be no sickness, no disease, no poverty, and no sorrow. There would be health, prosperity, and joy.

GOD IS ABLE TO DO MORE THAN YOU CAN ASK OR THINK

Again, God stands ready, willing, and able to answer your prayers. The apostle Paul summed up this reality when he said,

Now to Him who is able to do exceedingly abundantly above all that we ask or think, according to the power that works in us, to Him be glory in the church by Christ Jesus to all generations, forever and ever. Amen.
(Ephesians 3:20–21)

God is able to do exceedingly abundantly above all than you can ask or think, according to the power that works in you. Many people today are still asking, "Is it God's will to heal me?" or "Is it God's will to bless me financially?" or "Is it God's will for me to have the finances to be able to help others?" God has given us His will. His will is written in the words of the Bible. If the Bible says you can have something, this is the will of God for you.

YOUR HEAVENLY FATHER WANTS YOU TO ASK FOR GOOD THINGS

God wants you to ask for good things. He wants you to have the things that you need for your life. To receive them, you must seek and knock on the door of heaven. God has promised that when you seek, you will find. He will open the door of heaven and give you what you need.

> *Ask, and it will be given to you; seek, and you will find; knock, and it will be opened to you. For everyone who asks receives, and he who seeks finds, and to him who knocks it will be opened. Or what man is there among you who, if his son asks for bread, will give him a stone? Or if he asks for a fish, will he give him a serpent?*
> (Matthew 7:7–10)

God is a good God who wants to give good things to His children. The above passage does not give the impression that He wants you to be limited. On the contrary, He wants you to have whatever you need. Jesus used the illustration of bread to show the nature of what God desires to give you. Bread is important to daily life. It represents the essentials, what is important to you. Bread could be money, love, healing, joy, or anything else you need.

Again, that does not sound to me as if God wants you to be limited. Jesus said:

- Ask, and it will be given to you.
- Seek, and you will find.

- Knock, and it will be opened to you.
- Everyone who asks receives.
- He who seeks finds.
- To the one who knocks, the door will be opened!

The Bible says that just as a human father wants to provide for his children, our heavenly Father wants to provide many good things for His children.

If you then, being evil, know how to give good gifts to your children, how much more will your Father who is in heaven give good things to those who ask Him!

(Matthew 7:11)

If a child asks his father for bread, he will not give him a stone. If he asks him for fish, he will not give him a snake. If most earthly fathers want to give good things to their children, how much more does our heavenly Father want to give His children the good things they ask Him for! God is not trying to see how little He can do for you; He is trying to see how much He can do for you through your faith in His Word.

> GOD IS NOT TRYING TO SEE HOW LITTLE HE CAN DO FOR YOU; HE IS TRYING TO SEE HOW MUCH HE CAN DO FOR YOU.

WHAT'S YOUR MOTIVATION?

I have read many books and listened to many recorded teachings about prosperity. I have studied this information, and I have come to the conclusion that the purpose of prosperity is to enable us to finish the work that God has called us to do, and to be blessed in the process.

Your motive for prosperity should not be about amassing personal wealth and fortune for yourself. You cannot take your wealth with you when you die. Wealth is temporary; it is not eternal. It is only the good you do with your wealth that is eternal.

Our church spent several thousand dollars providing holiday dinners to more than five hundred people. Our money went toward a good cause, and we were glad to be able to spend it. The food met a temporary need, but it was our motivation that was important. God was pleased with the motivation of our hearts, and the results brought glory to Jesus.

Again, money has no intrinsic value. It is what you do with the money that is going to count for eternity. Having resources and money is important for finishing the work God has planned for you to do. You can be confident it is God's will to give you the money you need in order to fulfill what He has predestined and called you to complete.

If asking God for money bothers you, then begin by applying this principle to other areas of your life. Ask God for anything you need. Are you walking in all the love you want? Are you walking in all the peace you desire? Do you have all the joy you can hold? Do you need more of these things in your life? Of course you do. Everyone needs these things. Yet your motivation must be correct. The following are two improper and ineffective motivations for requesting something from God.

COVETOUSNESS

A man once walked up to me and said, "Your tie looks sharp. I just claim that tie." That is not faith. That is coveting, because it was my tie. God will not answer that prayer because the man desired someone else's possession, and God tells us not to covet. (See, for example, Romans 13:9.)

If I'd had that tie out on a rack for sale, or if I had been giving it away, he would have been able to claim it. He could not claim it as long as I was wearing it around my neck. You have to be honest, and you have to realize that you cannot go around coveting things that belong to other people. You cannot expect God to bless you when you are going against His will. God will not answer a prayer that is contrary to His Word, which expresses His will.

SELFISHNESS OR LUSTFULNESS

God also will not answer prayers that fulfill your lusts. You cannot ask God to give you things that you will use to gratify evil desires. You must ask God for good things. Fulfilling the "lusts of your flesh" is not a good thing. (See, for example, 1 Peter 4:1–3; 1 John 2:16–17.)

God's Word tells us to be led by the Holy Spirit. When the Holy Spirit leads you, you will not ask for things that go against God's will for your life.

You lust and do not have. You murder and covet and cannot obtain. You fight and war. Yet you do not have because you do not ask. You ask and do not receive, because you ask amiss, that you may spend it on your pleasures. (James 4:2–3)

In the above passage, the apostle James pointed out two problems. First, he said, *"You do not have because you do not ask."* Some people do not go to God humbly and ask for the things they need. Second, some people go to God but then pray selfishly. They ask for things for the wrong reasons. When you ask for the wrong reasons, God will not answer your prayers. Yet, if you find out what God has promised you, and if you ask for the right reasons, He will give you whatever you ask.

RECEIVE THE PROMISES OF GOD

There are thousands of promises in the Bible. God has given promises for every area of life. Relationships, jobs, money, health—you name it, and He has a promise for it. Every need humanity has ever had, or ever will have, is covered by God's promises in the Bible.

As we have seen, God has given us everything we need that pertains to our lives, and His promises are *"great and precious"*:

Grace and peace be multiplied to you in the knowledge of God and of Jesus our Lord, as His divine power has given to us all things that pertain to life and godliness, through the knowledge of Him who called us by glory and virtue, by which have been given to us exceedingly great and precious promises, that through these you may be partakers of

the divine nature, having escaped the corruption that is in the world through lust.
(2 Peter 1:2–4)

I wrote earlier that the Bible uses the past tense when it says that God *"has given to us all things that pertain to life and godliness."* He has already given us what we need.

> **THE MORE KNOWLEDGE YOU HAVE OF GOD, THE MORE YOU REALIZE WHAT ALREADY BELONGS TO YOU.**

The more knowledge you have of God, the more you realize what already belongs to you. He has called you to *"glory and virtue."* When you have what you need, you escape the corruption caused by lust. Having what you need helps you to remain pure and full of truth.

The promises of God are described as *"exceedingly great."* *Exceedingly* means "to an extreme degree." Exceedingly means without limits. God wants to bless you exceedingly, so that you might experience His divine nature. He wants you to escape the lustful corruption that is around you. He wants you to be like Jesus. He wants you to be blessed so you can be a blessing to others.

PRAY WITH CONFIDENCE IN GOD'S PROMISES

God's Word is His will, and the following verses mean what they say. These scriptural promises are not just for the apostles. They are for you today! Pray according to them when you ask God to meet your daily needs.

Most assuredly, I say to you, he who believes in Me, the works that I do he will do also; and greater works than these he will do, because I go to My Father. And whatever you ask in My name, that I will do, that the Father may be glorified in the Son. If you ask anything in My name, I will do it.

(John 14:12–14)

Most assuredly, I say to you, whatever you ask the Father in My name He will give you. Until now you have asked nothing in My name. Ask, and you will receive, that your joy may be full. (John 16:23–24)

So Jesus answered and said to them, "Have faith in God. For assuredly, I say to you, whoever says to this mountain, 'Be removed and be cast into the sea,' and does not doubt in his heart, but believes that those things he says will be done, he will have whatever he says. Therefore I say to you, whatever things you ask when you pray, believe that you receive them, and you will have them."

(Mark 11:22–24)

If you abide in Me, and My words abide in you, you will ask what you desire, and it shall be done for you. By this My Father is glorified, that you bear much fruit; so you will be My disciples. (John 15:7–8)

KNOW WHAT GOD PROMISES IN HIS WORD

You can ask God for whatever He has promised in His Word. You must not limit God and what He can do in you and through you. You have been given exceedingly great and precious promises.

What did God say you could have? What are some of these great and precious promises?

- SALVATION

For "whoever calls on the name of the Lord shall be saved." (Romans 10:13)

- DELIVERANCE FROM TROUBLE

Call upon Me in the day of trouble; I will deliver you, and you shall glorify Me.
(Psalm 50:15)

- FORGIVENESS

If we confess our sins, He is faithful and just to forgive us our sins and to cleanse us from all unrighteousness. (1 John 1:9)

- HEALING AND FORGIVENESS TO ANYONE WHO IS SICK IN THE CHURCH

Is anyone among you sick? Let him call for the elders of the church, and let them pray over him, anointing him with oil in the name of the Lord. And the prayer of faith will save the sick, and the Lord will raise him up. And if he has committed sins, he will be forgiven. (James 5:14–15)

- FREEDOM FROM FEAR, IN ADDITION TO POWER, LOVE, AND A SOUND MIND

For God has not given us a spirit of fear, but of power and of love and of a sound mind.
(2 Timothy 1:7)

- WISDOM

If any of you lacks wisdom, let him ask of God, who gives to all liberally and without reproach, and it will be given to him.
(James 1:5)

- VICTORY OVER COVETOUSNESS, DISCONTENT- MENT, AND LONELINESS

Let your conduct be without covetousness; be content with such things as you have. For He Himself has said, "I will never leave you nor forsake you." (Hebrews 13:5)

- PROSPERITY

Give, and it will be given to you: good mea- sure, pressed down, shaken together, and running over will be put into your bosom. For with the same measure that you use, it will be measured back to you.
(Luke 6:38)

- PEACE OF MIND, JOY, AND HOPE

Now may the God of hope fill you with all joy and peace in believing, that you may abound in hope by the power of the Holy Spirit. (Romans 15:13)

You can have any of the above promises; they are yours. God has given them to you, and you can stand in faith for them.

If you ask for anything according to His will, you know He hears you. Jesus said to ask the Father anything in His name, and He will give it to you. As far as I am concerned, it is hard to beat a deal like that!

CHAPTER NINE

REALIZING THE RICHES OF GOD'S RESOURCES

Y ou serve a God who is able to help you. You cannot ask for or think of anything greater than what He can do for you.

> *Now to Him who is able to do exceedingly abundantly above all that we ask or think, according to the power that works in us.*
> (Ephesians 3:20)

We limit ourselves when we say God will not bless us like He has blessed someone else. God is not like that. He will bless anyone who believes His promises. He does not show partiality; He does not have favorites. (See Romans 2:11.) God is able to do *"exceedingly abundantly"* for anyone who will not limit Him.

We limit God without realizing it when we do not think He can or will do something for us. Sometimes, we allow Him to bless us in certain areas of our lives but not in others. We do not expect God to do something for us, and so we do not receive it from Him. We do not ask, because we do not look beyond our limitations. We fail to recognize the *limitless abundance* of God.

RELEASING THE LIMITS ON GOD'S ABUNDANCE

The area in which many people find it hardest to receive the abundance of God is the area of finances. As soon as I start talking about the subject, I lose some people. They tune me out, thinking, *All that preacher ever wants to talk about is money. Those guys are just in this for the money.* This could not be further from the truth. I talk about money because money is important to God's work. Jesus said we are to put our treasure in a heavenly account. He indicated we are to store our treasure in heaven by giving toward the work of the ministry.

> *Lay up for yourselves treasures in heaven, where neither moth nor rust destroys and where thieves do not break in and steal. For where your treasure is, there your heart will be also.* (Matthew 6:20–21)

GOD IS MORE THAN ABLE TO MEET YOUR NEEDS *"ACCORDING TO HIS RICHES IN GLORY BY CHRIST JESUS"* (PHILIPPIANS 4:19).

Jesus spent much time talking about money. Financial matters are important to people, and Jesus used parables about money to illustrate principles in the kingdom of God. (See, for example, Matthew 18:23–35; Luke 15:8–10; 16:1–13; 19:12–27.) Jesus does not want you to trust in *"uncertain riches"* (1 Timothy 6:17).

Instead, you are to put your trust in Him. God is more than able to meet your needs *according to His riches in glory by Christ Jesus*" (Philippians 4:19).

We must understand that it is the power of God that brings us the money we need. *"And you shall remember the LORD your God, for it is He who gives you power to get wealth, that He may establish His covenant which He swore to your fathers, as it is this day"* (Deuteronomy 8:18). God is the source of your money supply, even though money comes to you through someone else's hands. God brings money to you through others when you are generous with what you possess. (See Luke 6:38.)

It is sad to see money stand between somebody and God. All too often, people will love the things of the world, and the things money will buy, instead of loving God and other people. When someone loves his money more than he loves God or other people, his priorities are out of order.

Money itself is not bad. Rather, the *love* of money is bad. (See 1 Timothy 6:10.) Money is necessary to live in this world. Jesus Himself paid taxes. (See Matthew 17:24–27.) He had a treasurer who carried around a money box. (See John 13:29.) And He was not without financial resources. Several wealthy women who were followers of Jesus supported His ministry. (See Luke 8:1–3.)

The Bible never says Jesus lived with a lack of finances. He had enough money for Judas to embezzle. (See John 12:4–6.) He had enough money that the disciples thought Judas was going out to help the poor when he was actually on his way to betray Jesus. (See John 13:27–29.) Jesus was not poor until

He made Himself spiritually and physically poor on the cross. Jesus' poverty on the cross enabled us to acquire spiritual and earthly riches to fulfill the purposes of God in our lives. *"For you know the grace of our Lord Jesus Christ, that though He was rich, yet for your sakes He became poor, that you through His poverty might become rich"* (2 Corinthians 8:9).

Money is not what is important. It is what you do with your money that is important. The reason you should allow God to bless you financially is that it takes money to spread the ministry of Jesus Christ around the world. When you are blessed financially, you can be generous in helping others. The apostle Paul collected a large combined offering from the churches in Greece for the church in Jerusalem to help the believers through some financial difficulties. He commended those who were eager to give to this offering. (See 2 Corinthians 9:1–15.)

DOING THE LORD'S WORK REQUIRES RESOURCES

We need to change our way of thinking about money. God's *"riches in glory by Christ Jesus"* (Philippians 4:19) apply to our finances, as well as to everything else we need. Money is necessary to help us fulfill the will of God for our lives and our mission to serve others. It allows us to accomplish what God has called us to do.

God allowed David to gather the resources to build a temple in Jerusalem. David made preparations for the place of worship that his son Solomon would build for the Lord. This temple was a magnificent work. It was built and adorned with an abundance of valuable gold, silver, brass, and the finest of cedar wood.

> *And David prepared iron in abundance for the nails of the doors of the gates and for the joints, and bronze in abundance beyond measure, and cedar trees in abundance; for the Sidonians and those from Tyre brought much cedar wood to David.*
>
> (1 Chronicles 22:3–4)

God provided an abundance of the supplies necessary to build the temple. This temple was where He would come down and dwell in the presence of His people. His glory would be in the innermost part of the temple. David described the extensive wealth he made available for the building project:

> *Indeed I have taken much trouble to prepare for the house of the LORD one hundred thousand talents of gold and one million talents of silver, and bronze and iron beyond measure, for it is so abundant. I have prepared timber and stone also, and you may add to them.*
>
> (verse 14)

One hundred thousand talents of gold! This is equivalent to 3,750 tons. At the current price of gold, it would be worth about $135 billion. The silver was one million talents, or 37,500 tons of silver. At today's prices, it would be worth about $29.7 billion. The total David gave was more than $164 billion. This did not include the cost of the brass and iron, which was too much to count. David's gift to the

Lord far surpassed the generosity of the wealthiest billionaires of our time.

When we talk about no more limits, therefore, we must always remember that the whole point is what God has called us to do, not money. If you do not understand that, you will run off and try to build yourself a fortune. The main focus should be doing the work of the Lord. David donated the best resources available in the world to build the temple. Nothing was too extravagant for God's purposes.

> *Moreover there are workmen with you in abundance: woodsmen and stonecutters, and all types of skillful men for every kind of work.* (1 Chronicles 22:15)

David provided timber in abundance to build the temple. We often do not think of things like timber as being money, yet David had to spend his money, or wealth, to obtain this timber. Today, you have to spend money on materials if you want to build a church or a television station. Most ministry projects involve money.

Jesus said the spiritual fields are ready for harvest, so we should pray for laborers. (See Luke 10:2.) We need laborers in the work of the ministry. How are those laborers going to live? With what funds are we going to pay them? How are ministries going to grow? How are we going to do anything for the Lord? We need money to fund almost everything we do.

Yet God has everything we need. He has the resources available to help you accomplish what needs to be done to fulfill His calling and purpose for your life.

David gave billions of dollars' worth of gold and silver from his own personal wealth, and he still had plenty left over to take care of his needs. You do not have to worry about yourself. When God blesses you with wealth, He gives you enough to accomplish His purposes and enough left over to take care of your needs.

The more you give to God, the more He makes available to you. This is a spiritual law. This is the law of seedtime and harvest, sowing and reaping, giving and receiving. If you are generous toward God, He will make sure you always have more than enough to give to every good work. (See 2 Corinthians 9:6–8.) God wants to bless us so that we can be a blessing. He wants us to abound in all areas of our lives so we can help others.

> GOD WANTS TO BLESS US SO THAT WE CAN BE A BLESSING.

There are no more limitations on the finances you need in order to do what God wants you to do. This truth is hard to comprehend, but you must try. You must dig into it until you truly understand it. Enter into the abundance of God for your finances so that you will be able to give generously to His work.

GOD'S NATURE IS UNLIMITED

One reason it is often difficult for us to understand concepts such as no more limitations on our finances is that we do not understand the limitless nature of God Himself. It takes time to reorient our minds and to eliminate the many misconceptions we have about Him. I have heard people say, "You never know what God is going to do. Sometimes He will bless you, and other times He will not." Such people are limited in their understanding of our God. They are blind to the promises in the Bible. The Scriptures have been given to us to equip us for service and to guide us through the difficulties of life.

All Scripture is given by inspiration of God, and is profitable for doctrine, for reproof, for correction, for instruction in righteousness, that the man of God may be complete, thoroughly equipped for every good work.
(2 Timothy 3:16–17)

The Bible gives us sound doctrine, or teaching, and keeps us in line with what God has planned for us. God wants us to correct our misunderstandings about Him so that we can be profitable in His service. The results of our understanding the purposes of God will be lives that are dedicated to doing good works for others. God's priority is to help people. We must always keep this truth in mind when we are trying to understand what God is calling us to do. He wants to give us the resources we need to accomplish His purpose of helping other people.

Again, God has given us His wonderful promise to do more than we could ask or think, to help us remove the limitations from our minds. He wants us to understand that He is not holding anything back from us. Do we really grasp the meaning of this promise? God is so much bigger and more powerful than we will ever imagine. We need to realize that no matter how big our problems seem to us, they are small in comparison to what God is able to do. His resources will always be more than enough for the task at hand.

Cleansing Our Minds with the Word of God

The problem is that we have been "brainwashed." We have allowed our brains to be washed with the wrong solution in trying to understand how to live our lives. As a result, we have been programmed to be selfish, and our minds have been limited to what we can imagine receiving for ourselves. This is not a proper motivation for receiving from God. The correct motivation is for us to understand the love of God and to respond to this love in a way that blesses the world.

Paul wrote that Jesus loved the church and gave Himself for it, so that He could cleanse the church with the water of the Word of God.

> *That He might sanctify and cleanse* [the church] *with the washing of water by the word, that He might present her to Himself a glorious church, not having spot or wrinkle or any such thing, but that she should be holy and without blemish.*
> (Ephesians 5:26–27)

How can we gain the proper motivation? By being cleansed by the Word of God. You must have your mind washed with the water of the Word. The Word will change you and the way you live—the way you think, the way you believe, the way you talk, and the way you walk.

> GOD WANTS US TO TAKE HOLD OF HIS PROMISES TO US, AND BEING CLEANSED BY THE WORD OF GOD WILL ENABLE US TO UNDERSTAND THESE PROMISES.

God wants us to take hold of His promises to us, and being cleansed by the Word of God will enable us to understand these promises. God is not limited. We are the ones who are limited. He wants our minds and bodies to be renewed so that we can be ready and able to serve Him and to serve a broken world. Our mission is to reach lost and hurting people and to tell them the good news of what Jesus has done for them. When we really understand what God has done for *us* through Jesus, then we will be more effective in reaching others.

God does not want us to be hindered in helping others to find out about His goodness. He wants us to be equipped to do many good works. We can be held back from doing these works by what we think, and this is why it is important for us to read and study the Bible. God's Word renews our minds so we can understand His unlimited nature and power. He has given us the Bible so we can understand what He wants from us and not be ignorant of His will.

What does He want from you? God wants you to serve Him with all that is within you. He wants you to be pure and holy and separated from the ways of the world, ways that are contrary to His nature. He desires for you to serve and obey Him. You start your service to God by dedicating yourself to understand and put into practice the principles outlined in His Word.

Paul eloquently summed up this dedication to serving God:

> *I beseech you therefore, brethren, by the mercies of God, that you present your bodies a living sacrifice, holy, acceptable to God, which is your reasonable service. And do not be conformed to this world, but be transformed by the renewing of your mind, that you may prove what is that good and acceptable and perfect will of God.*
> (Romans 12:1–2)

Many people's minds are closed and locked to the limitless nature of God. The world is always struggling against Him. The devil is the god of this world, and he has spun numerous webs of deceit that have sidetracked many people from understanding the true character of God. The worldly-minded Christian will never understand God's limitless nature. A person bound by worthless religious traditions will never fully experience God's limitless nature. Experiencing the limitless nature of God comes after you dedicate yourself to serving Him, after your mind has been renewed by the truth of the Bible, and after you have succeeded in applying its principles to your circumstances.

It Takes Time to Understand the Truth of "No More Limits"

Changing and renewing your mind is a process. It takes time to grasp the unlimited nature of God and His willingness to bless you exceedingly abundantly above all you can ask or think.

I have taught for years about the promises in the Bible. At times, I have had people come speak to me after a teaching, and I can tell by the way they talk or ask me a question that they do not understand what I have been saying. They may have listened to me for years, but they still do not understand how to apply what I have been teaching to their circumstances. It takes a while for some people to understand new ideas and principles. I am not being critical of these people. I am just saying it takes some people longer than others to learn things.

It took me two years to complete and pass a college algebra course, which was meant to be only a one-year course. Even after I passed it, I did not understand the material. I was glad when I finally finished that class. In addition, at one time, I was a psychology major and had to take statistics. That was another course I had a hard time understanding. The head of the psychology department taught the class, and I thought I was in a foreign country and that he was speaking a different language as he discussed "random sampling" and "statistical information." Just thinking about these terms reminds me of how uncomfortable the subject was for me years ago.

My point is that you can go to class and even pass but still know little to nothing about what you have been studying. The Word of God is like that for many people. They go to church and hear truth from God's Word, but they do not understand it. People hear things all the time and never put them into practice. The Word of God has to be put into practice if it is going to benefit you or those around you.

> THE WORD OF GOD HAS TO BE PUT INTO PRACTICE IF IT IS GOING TO BENEFIT YOU OR THOSE AROUND YOU.

You have to study the Bible for yourself. You have to dig into it in order to understand the concept of "no more limitations." Most people do not have any desire to dig into their Bibles until they find themselves in a crisis. Then, they are motivated to search their Bibles to learn what they need to know to survive.

THE SAINT BERNARD AND THE BEAGLES

We used to have a Saint Bernard dog named Eric. My wife, Jeanne, brought him home as a puppy. He was a precious little ball of fur, but he grew to be two hundred pounds. I thought I would make a house dog out of him until I heard a gnawing sound in the middle of the night. I went into the living room and saw that he had chewed the fabric off the arm of our couch—the leather, the foam rubber, everything—and was now gnawing on the wood. He had also regurgitated what he'd eaten all over the floor. That was the last time he was in the house. After this, he went outside to live for the rest of his life.

Our next-door neighbor had beagle dogs that barked at everything. If the wind blew, they barked;

if a leaf fell, they barked. When our dog Eric would walk around our yard, these beagles would stick their noses through a knothole in the fence and bark at him. And they would keep barking. Eric would become tired of this, so he would walk up to them, stick his nose in that knothole, and respond just once with his powerful-sounding bark. Immediately, the beagles would scatter.

Then, our neighbor built dog pens for his beagles, and one of the pens was next to the fence. One day, one of these little beagles wanted to see what was on the other side of the fence. I watched as he climbed on top of the pen next to the fence and jumped over into our yard. Our big Saint Bernard was lying there, and, all of a sudden, he saw the beagle.

Eric stood up and lumbered over to investigate the little dog. When the beagle saw this giant Saint Bernard coming toward him, he panicked, dove to the bottom of the fence, and began digging, trying to return to his side of the barrier. After he got about halfway under the fence, he became stuck. I could tell he thought the big dog was coming after him, because he started yelping and barking and digging with all four legs. He was doing all he could to get under that fence and return to where he belonged. Finally, he pushed himself through to the other side.

I share this story to illustrate a point: Some Christians seek the things of God only when they are stuck under the fence with their hind parts sticking out and the devil coming after them. At that point, they begin digging into the Bible furiously to find a way out of their situation. This is not the way things should be. You should dig into the Bible all the time.

Every day, you should be digging, digging, and digging to find out what God has promised you.

COMPREHENDING THE RICHES OF GOD'S LOVE

Throughout this book, I have quoted Ephesians 3:20. This Scripture is part of a prayer the apostle Paul prayed for the believers in Ephesus. This prayer is as applicable to us today as it was to them. It is one of the most eloquent prayers in the Bible. Read the entire prayer and try to comprehend all that is in it.

> *I bow my knees to the Father of our Lord Jesus Christ, from whom the whole family in heaven and earth is named, that He would grant you, according to the riches of His glory, to be strengthened with might through His Spirit in the inner man, that Christ may dwell in your hearts through faith; that you, being rooted and grounded in love, may be able to comprehend with all the saints what is the width and length and depth and height; to know the love of Christ which passes knowledge; that you may be filled with all the fullness of God. Now to Him who is able to do exceedingly abundantly above all that we ask or think, according to the power that works in us, to Him be glory in the church by Christ Jesus to all generations, forever and ever. Amen.*
> (Ephesians 3:14–21)

Paul prayed for the Ephesians to experience the love of God. When we are rooted and grounded in God's love, we can live victorious, overcoming lives.

Love is the spiritual foundation for our faith. God's love makes it possible for us to be filled with His fullness and to experience His doing exceeding abundantly above all that we can ask or think.

> WHEN YOU UNDERSTAND HOW MUCH GOD LOVES YOU AND WANTS TO BLESS YOU, IT SETS YOU FREE FROM THE LIMITATIONS AND BOUNDARIES THAT HINDER YOU.

Paul also prayed for the Ephesians to comprehend the love of God. When you understand how much God loves you and wants to bless you, it sets you free from the limitations and boundaries that hinder you. It enables you to realize your potential through God's power, which works in your inner being.

God loves you as much as He loves anyone else. You do not have to be "good enough" or do anything to deserve His love. You must understand that His love is what makes the benefits of an abundant life in Christ Jesus possible.

Because God loves you, no problem or situation can arise that will be greater than the resources He has for you. Once God's love is revealed to you, you will understand there are no more limits in Him.

THE RICHES OF GOD'S GLORY ARE AVAILABLE TO YOU

In the Ephesians 3 prayer, the apostle Paul used the phrase *"according to the riches of His glory"* (verse 16) to describe how Christ can dwell in our hearts by faith. *"According to the riches of His glory,"* we are grounded in love and obtain the fullness of God.

Paul also used a phrase similar to *"according to the riches of His glory"* when he wrote his letter to the Philippians:

> *And my God shall supply all your need according to His riches in glory by Christ Jesus.* (Philippians 4:19)

When Paul talked about the riches of God's glory, he wanted to communicate that there are no limits to what God can do. God can give you the ability to understand His love by the riches of His glory. He can let you know His fullness by the riches of His glory. And He can supply your needs by the riches of His glory.

The riches of God's glory are unlimited; there are no confines to what God can do for you spiritually, emotionally, physically, or financially. There is no limitation in your life that cannot be broken by the power of God's glory working in you through Christ Jesus. Nothing is too hard for God. There is not a single area of need in your life that cannot be met by the riches of His glory.

Renew your mind to what the Word of God says. Realize that the riches of God's glory make His unlimited resources available to meet all your needs. There is nothing to hinder the resources of God for your life!

CHAPTER TEN

WHOEVER IS BORN OF GOD OVERCOMES THE WORLD

We live in a fallen world, and there are evil spiritual forces that influence events in our lives. In the physical world, we cannot see electricity, but we can see its effects. Likewise, we cannot see the devil, but we can see the results of the evil he perpetrates in the world: Soldiers and civilians alike are killed in wars. Drunk drivers take the lives of other people. Innocent children die from cancer. Many destructive things in this world point to an evil force behind them.

In chapter 4, we discussed how God is good and does not use evil to tempt or teach His children. (See James 1:13.) Satan is *"the god of this world"* (2 Corinthians 4:4 KJV). He is the spirit behind crime, destruction, and death. But Jesus is the force behind life and all that is good. (See, for example, John 1:1–4; John 10:10; Galatians 5:22–23.)

The evil in the world cannot defeat a faith-filled Christian. The apostle John wrote about how our faith in God brings victory over the world:

> *For whatever is born of God overcomes the world. And this is the victory that has overcome the world; our faith.* (1 John 5:4)

Many limitations that we experience are imposed on us by the evil world in which we live. We exist in the midst of the world system, but we are not of the world. (See John 17:14–16.) We have to live here on earth, but we are not to be limited by the powers of darkness that are in control of the world system. By the power of God, we are to operate without limits in this world. We are more than conquerors and triumphant over the world through Christ.

THE SPIRITUAL FORCES AT WORK IN THE WORLD

To better understand how we can overcome the limits of the world, let us look behind the scenes and examine the spiritual forces at work. The origin of our struggle with evil involved the first human beings, Adam and Eve, who sinned against God and caused the human race to be separated from Him by their disobedience. (See Genesis 3.) Then, God sent Jesus into the world as a sinless Man. The Bible calls Jesus the *"last Adam"* (1 Corinthians 15:45). Because He never sinned, He earned the right to redeem humanity from the powers of darkness that came into the world when Adam and Eve disobeyed God. Jesus restored direct access to our heavenly Father. He made it possible once again for people to experience the divine nature of God in their lives. (See Romans 5.)

> **JESUS RESTORED DIRECT ACCESS TO OUR HEAVENLY FATHER.**

ADAM AND EVE LOST DOMINION OVER THE EARTH

Originally, God created a world of order where everything was good. (See Genesis 1.) He first created

Adam and placed him in the garden of Eden, which was a beautiful paradise. Adam was given dominion over the world and all the animals, birds, and fish. God and Adam walked together in this beautiful garden during the cool of the day. Adam was able to communicate directly with God and had fellowship with Him daily. God then created a woman, Eve, from Adam's side, so he would not be alone. God provided abundantly for Adam and Eve's needs. Man and woman lived in a place of perfect serenity and peace. They did not have to toil at their work, while pain, sickness, suffering, and death were unknown. God's will was done on earth as it was in heaven. (See Genesis 2.)

This picture-perfect setting did not last long, though, because there was a spiritual outlaw at work in the universe: Satan, or the devil. He himself had rebelled against God and been banished from heaven. (See, for example, Isaiah 14:12–15.) We have seen that the Bible describes him as the *"accuser"* (Revelation 12:10) and as a *"roaring lion, seeking whom he may devour"* (1 Peter 5:8). Jesus said,

> *The devil...was a murderer from the beginning, and does not stand in the truth, because there is no truth in him. When he speaks a lie, he speaks from his own resources, for he is a liar and the father of it.*
> (John 8:44)

Satan is subtle and crafty. He does not immediately make his presence known but operates cunningly behind the scenes. The devil came into this picture of perfection in the garden of Eden with a plan to steal, kill, and destroy. (See John 10:10.) As I wrote earlier, he disguised himself in the form of a serpent, which must have been, at that time, a beautiful creature. Eve was walking in the garden, and the beautiful creature began to talk to this innocent woman. (See Genesis 3:1–5.)

God had placed two special trees in the garden of Eden. There were (1) the tree of the knowledge of good and evil, and (2) the tree of life. God had told Adam he could eat of any tree in the garden except for the tree of the knowledge of good and evil.

> *And the LORD God commanded the man, saying, "Of every tree of the garden you may freely eat; but of the tree of the knowledge of good and evil you shall not eat, for in the day that you eat of it you shall surely die."* (Genesis 2:16–17)

The serpent succeeded in tempting Eve to disobey God. She fell for his trickery and ate fruit from the forbidden tree. She then gave the fruit to her husband, and he ate, as well. (See Genesis 3:6.)

The consequence of their disobedience was that they immediately lost their innocence; they now had a sinful nature. Their disastrous decision has affected all of humanity from that time to today. God banished Adam and Eve from the garden of Eden to prevent them from eating from the tree of life and living forever with a spiritually dead nature.

Adam and Eve lost their paradise and experienced hardship, suffering, and death. They forfeited their right to have dominion over the earth and the animals. They had to toil in their work in order to survive. (See Genesis 3:16–24.) As a result of their actions, through which sin entered into the world, the world has been in turmoil ever since.

Jesus Regained Dominion Over the Earth

Yet God was not finished with humanity. He had a plan to "buy us back," or redeem us, from our sins. The Bible is the story of His plan to redeem humanity. Jesus is the cornerstone of God's plan of redemption. (See Acts 4:10–12.) God sent His perfect Son to die for an imperfect world. Jesus' death on the cross paid the penalty for our sins. Through Jesus, we are set free from the power of sin and the power of the devil. (See Acts 26:18.)

The first Adam failed the test of the devil. But Jesus, the last Adam, passed all the temptations and tests of the devil. And, His death on the cross made it possible for us to have direct access to the Father again. His victory over death was a triumph over all evil. As we discussed in chapter 2, He has made it possible for us to share in His triumph over the evil in the world. (See 2 Corinthians 2:14.)

Before Jesus was about to be crucified and die on the cross, He prayed that His followers would be kept from Satan and the evil in the world:

> *I do not pray that You should take them out of the world, but that You should keep them from the evil one.* (John 17:15)

God has a plan for His children. He wants us to remain in the world to do His bidding. One day, Jesus will return to earth to restore the peace and harmony that existed in the garden of Eden. He has promised He will return. (See, for example, Revelation 21:3–5; 22:12.) However, until Jesus returns, we are expected to do great deeds in His name and to bring Him glory.

JESUS IS IN CHARGE OF THE UNIVERSE, AND HE HAS GIVEN US HIS AUTHORITY TO CARRY OUT HIS PLAN FOR THE WORLD.

Jesus' last words to His disciples were instructions to go and take His message to the world. He told them He had been given authority and dominion over heaven and earth. Jesus is in charge of the universe, and He has given us His authority to carry out His plan for the world. He wants us to glorify His Father in the world and to demonstrate that the devil has been defeated; his dominion over the earth is no more.

And Jesus came and spoke to them, saying, "All authority has been given to Me in heaven and on earth. Go therefore and make disciples of all the nations, baptizing them in the name of the Father and of the Son and of the Holy Spirit, teaching them to observe all things that I have commanded you; and lo, I am with you always, even to the end of the age." (Matthew 28:18–20)

And He said to them, "Go into all the world and preach the gospel to every creature. He who believes and is baptized will be saved; but he who does not believe will be condemned. And these signs will follow those who believe: In My name they will cast out demons; they will speak with new tongues; they will take up serpents; and if they drink anything deadly, it will by no means hurt them; they will lay hands on the sick, and they will recover." (Mark 16:16–18)

SHARING THE LIGHT OF THE WORLD

The great apostle John said that if we are born of God, we can overcome the world.

For whatever is born of God overcomes the world. And this is the victory that has overcome the world; our faith. (1 John 5:4)

The Greek word that John used for *"world"* is *kosmos. Kosmos* can refer to planet Earth, or it can refer to the world of darkness—in other words, the evil world that stands in opposition to the kingdom of God.

When Adam sinned, he relinquished his God-given authority to Satan. That is when Satan became the *"god of this world"* (2 Corinthians 4:4 KJV). Jesus has taken away the power of the god of this world. However, Satan continues to keep most people in darkness by his lies. Jesus came as the light of the world, and He has sent us out to share His light with those who are in darkness. (See, for example, John 12:46; Matthew 5:14–16.) We are sent to proclaim truth to those who are bound. We are sent to free these people from the kingdom of darkness and to spread the good news of the kingdom of God. (See, for example, Acts 26:17–18.)

The apostle Paul acknowledged the existence of powers of darkness. In Ephesians, he said we struggle against evil spiritual forces:

> *For we do not wrestle against flesh and blood, but against principalities, against powers, against the rulers of the darkness of this age, against spiritual hosts of wickedness in the heavenly places.*
>
> (Ephesians 6:12)

The word in the original Greek for *"rulers"* is *kosmokrator*, meaning "world ruler." It is a reference to Satan.

Paul also painted a picture of a spiritual soldier doing battle against the rulers and powers of darkness. (See Ephesians 6:13–18.) The world of darkness is real, but God has equipped us with all we need to live victoriously and to overcome that darkness.

Jesus conquered Satan and destroyed his ability to deceive, because the Holy Spirit dwelling within us gives us spiritual discernment to know good from evil, and He guides us into all truth. (See, for example, John 16:13–14.) Jesus has given us the ability to operate in victory and to be overcomers in the midst of a chaotic world. When you have been born of God, you have the potential to be victorious over all the powers of darkness in this world.

Adverse circumstances in the world can be overcome. For example, if a doctor uses science to measure the limitations of your body, and he finds cancer or another disease, you can go to the Word of God and discover that you can overcome it.

The circumstances of the world may set limits on you, but this does not mean they cannot be changed. You can move the perimeters. You can overcome your limitations and unleash heaven's blessings with the help of God.

Too often, we set boundaries for ourselves, or we let others set them for us. This is a practice we need to quit. We need to stop setting limitations, and we need to stop allowing other people to set limits on us that are contrary to the will of God.

HE WHO IS IN YOU IS GREATER THAN HE WHO IS IN THE WORLD

Jesus told His disciples,

These things I have spoken to you, that in Me you may have peace. In the world you will have tribulation; but be of good cheer, I have overcome the world.   (John 16:33)

Our Savior overcame the limits of the world, and He told His disciples He was an overcomer so that they would have joy. He did not say they wouldn't have difficulties. He said they would have problems in the world but that they could find peace and joy in Him because He had overcome the world.

It is easy for us to see Jesus as an overcomer, but it is sometimes hard to see ourselves as over-comers. All of us have failed to live up to our fullest potential. However, our present situation does not mean the Word of God is not true. The apostle John wrote, *"Whatever is born of God overcomes the world"* (1 John 5:4). If you are a Christian, you have the ability within you to overcome the power and limitations of the world.

As I wrote earlier, you have the greatness of the Holy Spirit within you. His power gives you the ability to overcome the world and its limitations. In the apostle John's day, there were some false prophets who were bothering some of his spiritual children. (See 1 John 4:1–6.) These believers apparently struggled against the false teachers and won a victory in their lives. After their triumph of faith, John said to them,

> *You are of God, little children, and have overcome them, because He who is in you is greater than he who is in the world.*
>
> (verse 4)

When we follow the inner leading and urging of the Holy Spirit, we fulfill God's will for our lives and bring glory to Him. (See John 16:5–15.) All Christians have God's power within them, and we need to recognize this power and apply it to all our situations and circumstances. The Holy Spirit gives us power over the limitations of the world.

> JESUS DEFEATED THE EVIL GOD OF THIS WORLD. WE HAVE THE RIGHT TO ENJOY THE BENEFITS OF HIS VICTORY OVER THE DEVIL.

We can be full of joy because Jesus defeated the evil god of this world. We have the right to enjoy the benefits of His victory over the devil. The strength and power of God are within us, and we can be victorious over any limitations the world of darkness throws at us.

Again, the Bible is full of amazing promises, and we have to go out of our way to misunderstand what it says. Before He returned to the Father, Jesus spoke plainly to His disciples, giving them instructions to carry on His ministry. He also expanded the limitations of their work.

> *Most assuredly, I say to you, he who believes in Me, the works that I do he will do also; and greater works than these he will do, because I go to My Father. And whatever you ask in My name, that I will do, that the Father may be glorified in the Son. If you ask anything in My name, I will do it.*
>
> (John 14:12–14)

Some people will try to explain away these words of Jesus, attempting to prove with many arguments why His words applied only to His disciples and are no longer true today. They all agree they were true when Jesus was here on earth, but they say they are not for us now.

Jesus' words do apply to us today. He never intended for His works to stop with the death of the disciples. In fact, church history records many miracles and signs throughout the centuries since the time of Christ. Even today, there are many documented reports of miracles occurring around the world. Jesus has not changed; "[He] *is the same yesterday, today, and forever*" (Hebrews 13:8).

Jesus instructed His disciples to teach others what He had taught them. He laid down the principles, and He expected them to teach those who would follow. Read the words of Jesus again. As you read, realize that, if you are a believer in Jesus, these words apply to you:

> *Most assuredly, I say to you, he who be-*
> *lieves in Me, the works that I do he will do*
> *also; and greater works than these he will*
> *do, because I go to My Father. And whatever*
> *you ask in My name, that I will do, that the*
> *Father may be glorified in the Son. If you*
> *ask anything in My name, I will do it.*
>
> (John 14:12–14)

Do you believe in Jesus? Do you believe He spoke these words to all who believe in Him? Then, do not believe the nonsense of those who claim these words no longer mean what they say. If you believe in Jesus, you can do the works that He did. Jesus promises that you can ask anything in His name, and He will do it, so that the Father will be glorified in Him.

Because Jesus left us the power of His name, we can stand in the face of sickness, disease, poverty, and demons. At the sound of the wonderful name of Jesus in the mouths of believers, sickness, disease, poverty, and demons must flee.

> *Let this mind be in you which was also in*
> *Christ Jesus, who, being in the form of God,*
> *did not consider it robbery to be equal with*
> *God, but made Himself of no reputation, tak-*
> *ing the form of a bondservant, and coming*
> *in the likeness of men. And being found in*
> *appearance as a man, He humbled Himself*
> *and became obedient to the point of death,*
> *even the death of the cross. Therefore God*
> *also has highly exalted Him and given Him*
> *the name which is above every name, that at*
> *the name of Jesus every knee should bow,*

of those in heaven, and of those on earth,
and of those under the earth, and that every
tongue should confess that Jesus Christ is
Lord, to the glory of God the Father.

(Philippians 2:5–11)

Everything that has a name must bow on its knee to the name of Jesus. The name of cancer has to bow its knee to Jesus. Heart disease has to bow its knee to Jesus. Poverty and lack have to bow their knees to Jesus. At the sound of the name of Jesus, *everything* must bow.

All power in heaven and on earth has been given to Jesus, and He has granted us the right to use His name to the glory of God. Through His name, we can do great and mighty works. There is no power on earth or in heaven that can stand against the power of the name of Jesus. There is no limitation that can stand against that name. His name is a potent force for overcoming limits in our lives.

> THE NAME OF JESUS IS A POTENT FORCE FOR OVERCOMING LIMITS IN OUR LIVES.

We must recognize that the name of Jesus is still as powerful and effective today as it was in the days of the early church. As a believer, you have the right to use Jesus' name to break through any barriers and to expand the scope of His ministry to those around you.

When you accept Jesus Christ as Lord of your life, you become a member of a spiritual kingdom, the kingdom of heaven. You have rights and privileges that are granted to you above and beyond what you can understand or imagine.

Jesus had some wonderful things to say about those who are least in the kingdom of heaven.

> *Assuredly, I say to you, among those born of women there has not risen one greater than John the Baptist; but he who is least in the kingdom of heaven is greater than he.*
> (Matthew 11:11)

The least person in the kingdom of heaven is greater than John the Baptist, one of the greatest people ever born. How could that be? Let us revisit two verses we have looked at before.

> *Yet in all these things we are more than conquerors through Him who loved us.*
> (Romans 8:37)

> *I can do all things through Christ who strengthens me.* (Philippians 4:13)

Through the work of Jesus Christ, Christians can operate without limitations, as far as the will of God is concerned. God has not held back anything from you. He wants you to take advantage of your rights in the kingdom of heaven to glorify Him in the world.

GLORIFYING GOD IN THE WORLD

The spiritual power given to a Christian is immeasurable. The power of God is available to you to destroy the limitations of the world. This is a fantastic privilege. God's power will enable you have many victories over the powers of darkness around you. However, when you see the demons fleeing at the name of Jesus and your limits being broken, do not rejoice because you have power over the devil. Rejoice because you belong to God and to His kingdom.

DEFLECT ALL PERSONAL GLORY TO THE LORD

Behold, I give you the authority to trample on serpents and scorpions, and over all the power of the enemy, and nothing shall by any means hurt you. Nevertheless do not rejoice in this, that the spirits are subject to you, but rather rejoice because your names are written in heaven.   (Luke 10:19–20)

We should not glory in the fact that the devil is subject to us. We should not glory in the fact that we are superior to the forces of evil in the world. If there is anything we can glory in, it is in the glory of Jesus. The only things worth glorying in are the death and triumph of Jesus on the cross.

But God forbid that I should boast except in the cross of our Lord Jesus Christ, by whom the world has been crucified to me, and I to the world.   (Galatians 6:14)

Through his power and authority in Christ, the apostle Paul put things into perspective with the above words. We should not glory in our authority over evil. We should not glory in our ability to overcome our limitations. We should not glory in anything in the world. Our only glory should be in the Savior of the world, Jesus Christ. Let everything be done for the glory of God and His Son.

KEEP YOUR PRIORITIES STRAIGHT

To glorify God in the world, it is important to have the proper priorities. The fact that you can overcome limitations is not the most important thing in life. You need to overcome your limitations, but the most important thing is to have a loving relationship with Jesus Christ and to share that love with others.

The apostle Paul had a good word about priorities:

> *Yet indeed I also count all things loss for the excellence of the knowledge of Christ Jesus my Lord, for whom I have suffered the loss of all things, and count them as rubbish, that I may gain Christ.* (Philippians 3:8)

You have many rights and privileges in Christ. God has given you His power and authority. He has provided you with everything you need to live victoriously over your circumstances. Yet none of these things is as important as knowing Jesus as your Lord. And loving God and His Son Jesus are more important than anything else. Love should be the strongest force operating in your life. Jesus said,

> *The first of all the commandments is: "Hear, O Israel, the LORD our God, the LORD is one. And you shall love the LORD your God with*

all your heart, with all your soul, with all your mind, and with all your strength." This is the first commandment. And the second, like it, is this: "You shall love your neighbor as yourself." There is no other commandment greater than these. (Mark 12:29–31)

As we love the Lord and love one another, we advance the kingdom of God on earth, demonstrate His dominion in this world, and bring Him glory!

Chapter Eleven

Overcoming Satan and the World System

T he book of Revelation describes two ways to overcome the devil and the power of the world system:

> *And they overcame* [Satan] *by the blood of the Lamb and by the word of their testimony, and they did not love their lives to the death.* (Revelation 12:11)

The above Scripture gives us insight into living a life without limitations—an overcoming, victorious life. We overcome (1) *"by the blood of the Lamb"* and (2) *"by the word of* [our] *testimony."* We need to understand our redemption in Christ and the importance of the words we speak, which are our testimony to the world.

There is a vital connection between the blood of Jesus and our redemption from the world and the powers of darkness. When we are in heaven, we will hear praises being sung about Jesus' blood.

> *And they sang a new song, saying: "You are worthy to take the scroll, and to open*

> *its seals; for You were slain, and have re-*
> *deemed us to God by Your blood out of every*
> *tribe and tongue and people and nation."*
>   (Revelation 5:9)

Jesus is worthy to receive our praises. He is the One who died and redeemed us by His blood from the powers of darkness. He will receive well-deserved praise and adoration from those of us whom He has redeemed from all the nations and peoples of the world.

It is important for you to give proper testimony regarding what Jesus has done for you. You can overcome the devil by the word of your testimony. Note that Jesus said you will be accountable for every word you speak:

> *But I say to you that for every idle word*
> *men may speak, they will give account of it*
> *in the day of judgment. For by your words*
> *you will be justified, and by your words you*
> *will be condemned.*   (Matthew 12:36–37)

Understanding how you overcome by the blood of the Lamb and by the word of your testimony will help you to further see how you can have victory over the limitations of the world. You live in the world, but you are not of the world. (See John 17:14–16.) Anything you can learn about overcoming the limitations of the world will help you to triumph over your

GOD WANTS YOU TO THROW OFF THE LIMITS THAT KEEP YOU FROM BEING ALL THAT HE WANTS YOU TO BE.

circumstances. God wants you to throw off the limits that keep you from being all that He wants you to be. And the blood of Jesus and the words you speak are important keys to helping you walk in victory over the limitations of the world.

Overcoming Limitations by the Blood of the Lamb

The Significance of Blood Sacrifices

In our contemporary society, blood sacrifices are no longer a part of everyday life. Yet, in Old Testament times, blood sacrifices were regularly offered, and they were better understood. God established blood sacrifices as a way for His people to receive forgiveness for their sins prior to the coming of Jesus Christ. His justice was satisfied when the blood of an innocent animal—a symbol of Christ—was shed and offered as a penalty for sin.

Not just any animal would do for blood sacrifices. Only certain animals and birds were acceptable for them. God established laws and regulations for presenting animal sacrifices and other offerings. He established the priesthood to tend to these sacrifices and offerings, and He gave strict guidelines for the ways in which the priests could approach Him. Priests could not minister before God as they pleased. They could approach Him only in certain ways prescribed by the law of Moses. (See Exodus 19–24.) Priests died when they failed to follow God's commandments concerning sacrifices and offerings. (See, for example, Leviticus 10:1–2.)

The nation of Israel had several major holidays that involved an elaborate series of feasts and blood sacrifices. One such holiday was known as the Passover. This celebration commemorated the Israelites' deliverance from slavery in Egypt. Right before they left Egypt, the Israelite families were each commanded to sacrifice a lamb and to put its blood upon the doorframe of their home.

God's judgment was going to come on all those who were living in Egypt who did not have the blood of a lamb smeared on their doorframes. The judgment would be in the form of a destroying angel who would kill the firstborn of each household—both people and livestock. But the destroying angel would pass over the houses where the blood had been placed around the doorframes and would not kill the firstborn of the Israelites or their animals. This was the significance of the Feast of Passover. God's judgment came upon the Egyptians, but His judgment and wrath passed over the Israelites. (See Exodus 12:21–23, 28–30.)

After all the firstborn of the Egyptians were killed, the Egyptians were more than ready to allow the Israelites to leave their country. When the Israelites left, the Egyptians gave them their gold, silver, livestock, and other wealth and hurriedly sent them on their way. (See verses 35–36.) Not only did the Israelites take the wealth of the Egyptians, but they also obtained a promise of good health from the Lord. (See Exodus 15:26.)

God redeemed His chosen people from slavery in Egypt. He took them into the desert and miraculously provided for their needs. He caused water to come from rocks and manna to come down from heaven every day as food. Over two million people were sustained in this desert environment for forty years. (See Deuteronomy 2:7.) God spoke to the Israelites' leader, Moses, and delivered His laws to them. Through Moses, God also established the procedures for blood sacrifices and holy days.

The first five books of the Bible tell of the early history of Israel and the establishment of the Jewish religion. The Jewish nation and religion were essential in God's plan to redeem humanity from sin, sickness, disease, and poverty. The deliverance of Israel from slavery in Egypt was symbolic of God's provision of redemption for the entire human race through Jesus Christ.

The animal sacrifices of the Old Testament point to the centerpiece of salvation in the New Testament: Jesus dying on the cross for the sins of the world. The shedding of animals' blood in the sacrifices was the forerunner of the shedding of the blood of Jesus.

THE IMPORTANCE OF BLOOD COVENANTS

The blood covenant is an important theme underlying the entire Bible. The Old Testament and the New Testament are based on covenants between God and His people. The word *testament* means "covenant," which is a very involved form of contract. A marriage relationship is a covenant relationship. There is the legal aspect of it, but there is much more as far as the relationship is concerned.

Blood covenants were common in ancient times. They were well understood as ways to seal agreements. In Genesis, Abram (whose name was later changed to Abraham) entered into a blood covenant with God in which he sacrificed animals and birds. God promised Abram a child from the seed of his own body. He also promised him in Genesis 15:18 that the land *"from the river of Egypt* [the Nile] *to the great river, the River Euphrates"* would be given to his descendants. (See Genesis 15.) Later, God confirmed His blood covenant with Abram and commanded him to be circumcised, along with every male in his household. Circumcision was another form of blood covenant. At this time, God changed Abram's name to Abraham and his wife's name from Sarai to Sarah, while declaring that the promised child would come through Sarah. (See Genesis 17.)

Israel's priests made daily animal sacrifices as part of another blood covenant God established, based on the law given to Moses, which we discussed briefly above. God pronounced blessings and curses upon this covenant relationship. If the Israelites followed the blood covenant, they would thrive and prosper. If they disobeyed the blood covenant, they would be scattered into the surrounding nations and suffer persecution. (See Deuteronomy 27–30.)

Later, God established a covenant with King David and promised him that he would produce an Heir and King who would endure forever, and we know that this Heir shed His blood on the cross for us. (See 2 Samuel 7.) King David was a descendant of Abraham, and Jesus was a descendant of King David. (See, for example, Matthew 1:1–16.) Jesus was born into a line of people who had established blood covenant relationships with God. He was born at a time when Israel offered daily blood sacrifices in the temple. He came and fulfilled the blood covenant obligations of Abraham, Moses, and David perfectly. (See Hebrews 10:1–18.) He was the fulfillment of all the blood covenant promises ever made by God to people of faith. (See Acts 13:26–39; Romans 4:3–18.)

Jesus established a new blood covenant sealed with His own blood, which was shed for us. (See, for example, Luke 22:17–20.) Our tradition of Communion is symbolic of the new blood covenant Jesus established.

When you accept Jesus as Lord, therefore, you enter into a blood covenant relationship with Him. When you obey the commandments of God and love Him, you are blessed with the privileges of the new blood covenant. The blood of Jesus Christ seals our victory and triumph over our limitations. Jesus was known as the Lamb that was slain for the sins of the world. (See John 1:29; Revelation 13:8.) He was the final sacrifice. All the animal sacrifices under the old covenant were completed by the one sacrifice of Jesus Christ. (See Hebrews 10:8–12.)

> **THE BLOOD OF JESUS CHRIST SEALS OUR VICTORY AND TRIUMPH OVER OUR LIMITATIONS.**

The statement from Revelation about overcoming by the blood of the Lamb is a reference to our redemption in Christ. Jesus paid the penalty for our sins, and He fulfilled all the obligations of the old blood covenants. (See Romans 10:4.)

With His Blood, Jesus Redeemed Us from the Curse of the Law

As I wrote earlier, the old blood covenant included both blessings and curses. Sickness, disease, and poverty were among the curses of the old covenant. (See Deuteronomy 28:15–68.) Yet Jesus' death redeemed us from these curses.

> *Christ has redeemed us from the curse of the law, having become a curse for us (for it is written, "Cursed is everyone who hangs on a tree"), that the blessing of Abraham might come upon the Gentiles in Christ Jesus, that we might receive the promise of the Spirit through faith.* (Galatians 3:13–14)

The blessings are all that remain now that Jesus has done away with the curses. We have rights and privileges under the new blood covenant that include the blessings of the law. (See Deuteronomy 28:1–14.) These blessings go beyond spiritual blessings; they involve health and prosperity. You cannot separate health and prosperity from the blessings of the Old Testament blood covenants: salvation, health, and prosperity were all part of the blood-covenant package.

The Communion we take, with the wine or grape juice to represent the blood of Jesus, is to remind us that Jesus has redeemed us from the power of the devil. Just as the Passover was celebrated by the Jews to commemorate their deliverance from slavery, we are to celebrate Communion as a reminder that we have been redeemed from the powers of darkness.

We have been redeemed from sin, sickness, and poverty by the blood of Jesus.

Our redemption by Jesus' blood includes freedom from the bondage of the limits imposed on us by the devil. Satan comes to steal, kill, and destroy, but we have been redeemed from his power because we have a powerful blood covenant relationship with Jesus. We stand in victory over the power of the enemy by the blood of the Lamb.

OVERCOMING LIMITATIONS BY THE WORD OF YOUR TESTIMONY

We have looked at what it means to be redeemed by the blood of the Lamb. Let us now look at the second part of Revelation 12:11 and what it means to overcome the devil and the world system by the word of our testimony.

> *And they overcame* [Satan]...*by the word of their testimony, and they did not love their lives to the death.* (Revelation 12:11)

THERE IS A PRICE TO PAY FOR BEING AN OVERCOMER

Notice that at the end of the above verse, it says, *"They did not love their lives to the death."* This statement in Revelation refers to overcomers as people who are willing to give up their lives for their testimonies.

How many Christians today are willing to die for what they believe? When the book of Revelation was written, if you were a follower of Jesus Christ, you put your life at risk. Today, people are still killed for being followers of Christ. In some countries, Christians have been beheaded for sharing their faith. Others are harshly persecuted for their beliefs.

Most Christians living in free countries are not faced with intense persecution. However, the Bible says that a time of great tribulation will come upon the world. During this time, all people will be forced to make a decision. They will have to choose between serving Jesus and serving the Antichrist (also called the Beast)—a world leader in league with the devil. If they will not forsake Jesus and His words, they will face tremendous persecution. They will be unable to buy or sell without the mark of the Antichrist. (See Revelation 13:16–17.) They will face hunger, thirst, sorrow, and death. (Contrast Revelation 7:9–17.)

Are you willing to risk your life for your testimony that Jesus is your Lord and Savior? Are you willing to die for what you believe? There is a price to be paid for being a Christian. Do you really want to be an overcomer? Is the cost too much to bear? How willing are you to share your testimony and faith with others?

> YOU CAN OVERCOME THE WORLD BY BEING A WITNESS TO WHAT JESUS HAS DONE.

You can overcome the world by being a witness to what Jesus has done. You have to act on Jesus' words and be obedient to the calling of God on your life. This is what it takes to be an overcomer. You must speak God's words and be a living witness of His grace and glory. You must not be ashamed of Jesus, who left a solemn warning to those who would be ashamed of Him and His words:

For whoever is ashamed of Me and My words, of him the Son of Man will be ashamed when He comes in His own glory, and in His Father's, and of the holy angels.
(Luke 9:26)

There is power in sharing the good news of Jesus with other people. There is power in speaking the Word of God over your life and the lives of others. The apostle Paul said he was not ashamed to testify about Jesus. Everywhere Paul went, he preached and taught about the power of Jesus Christ. His proclaimed his message boldly, and he was willing to suffer and die, if necessary, for what he believed.

For I am not ashamed of the gospel of Christ, for it is the power of God to salvation for everyone who believes, for the Jew first and also for the Greek. (Romans 1:16)

Paul was an overcomer. He overcame the devil by the blood of the Lamb and by the word of his testimony. What kinds of things did he face? He was stoned and left for dead. (See Acts 14:19–20.) He was whipped—not just once but five times. (See 2 Corinthians 11:24.) He was willing to pay a price for living a life without limits. He was willing to do whatever was necessary to be an overcomer and bring glory to God. He lived a life of faith, and He encouraged others to follow his example.

The power to be a witness of Christ and an overcomer is available to you because you are redeemed by the blood of Jesus. God can strengthen you in your weaknesses. Jesus said His followers would receive power to be His witnesses in their cities, their nations, and throughout the earth.

> *But you shall receive power when the Holy*
> *Spirit has come upon you; and you shall be*
> *witnesses to Me in Jerusalem, and in all*
> *Judea and Samaria, and to the end of the*
> *earth.* (Acts 1:8)

You should therefore not be ashamed to speak up for Christ. You must be willing to stake your life on the Word of God and be a witness filled with the power of the Holy Spirit. This type of faith is the kind that will move mountains and overcome all the attacks of the devil.

EVERY WORD YOU SPEAK SHOULD BRING GLORY TO GOD

I mentioned earlier that Jesus talked about the importance of everything you say. The words you speak either justify or condemn you.

> *But I say to you that for every idle word*
> *men may speak, they will give account of it*
> *in the day of judgment. For by your words*
> *you will be justified, and by your words you*
> *will be condemned.* (Matthew 12:36–37)

Does your testimony glorify God? Your words should be chosen carefully to give Him glory. The words you use every day are part of your testimony. What is that testimony going to be? What ideas and attitudes are you going to convey? Are you going to speak the words of the world, or are you going to speak the words of God?

- If the world says, "You are sick," your testimony should be, "I am healed by the stripes of Jesus." (See 1 Peter 2:24.)

- If the world says, "What you did is unforgiveable," your testimony should be, "My sins are forgiven, and I am clean before God." (See 1 John 1:9.)

- If the world says, "You should worry about having enough money for groceries and clothes," your testimony should be, "I will not worry about what I will eat or wear. I will seek first the kingdom of God, and these things will be given to me by my heavenly Father." (See Matthew 6:25–34.)

- If the world says, "You should be afraid," your testimony should be, "I will not live in fear, because God has not given me a spirit of fear; He has given me a spirit of power, love, and a sound mind." (See 2 Timothy 1:7.)

- If the world says, "You are worthless," your testimony should be, "I am valuable, because I was bought at a price. I belong to God, and I will glorify Him." (See 1 Corinthians 6:20.)

Whatever the world throws at you, you can overcome by the blood of the Lamb and the word of your testimony. The Word of God is greater than any of your circumstances. Circumstances can be changed, but the Word of God cannot be changed. Agree with the Word of God rather than with your situation. Build your life on the

BUILD YOUR LIFE ON THE SOLID ROCK OF THE FAITH-FILLED WORDS OF JESUS.

solid rock of the faith-filled words of Jesus, not on the shifting sands of life's circumstances and feelings. If you believe the Word of God is true, you will speak the Word of God. You either believe God's Word is true, or you believe your circumstances are true. When the two do not agree, you should always believe the Word of God. That should be all there is to it.

The Benefits of Overcoming the World

Many of us have seen commercials that claim owning a particular charge card has its advantages. Possessors of these cards are portrayed as having recognition and purchasing power. The cards are marketed in such a way as to appeal to people's pride, implying that if you own one of these cards, you will be seen as successful.

I can tell you that owning a charge card is not the key to a successful life. Being an overcomer in Jesus Christ is the key to a successful life! You have a heavenly account, and God is keeping track of what you do with what He has given you. You will be rewarded for your works.

> *And behold, I am coming quickly, and My reward is with Me, to give to every one according to his work.* (Revelation 22:12)

Jesus is going to return soon to judge the world. (See, for example, Acts 17:30–31.) Those who do not believe in Him will be condemned. To those who do believe in Him, He will grant everlasting life. Those who believe in Him will receive the benefits of being overcomers.

The apostle John wrote the last words of Jesus recorded in the Bible, which are found in the book of Revelation. Revelation was originally delivered to various first-century churches, each of which received specific words from Jesus. Several times, Jesus mentioned benefits that would be given to those who were overcomers. If you are a Christian, you are an overcomer, and these promises are for you. You need to pay close attention to what Jesus was saying to the churches.

You Will Eat from the Tree of Life

Our Lord said,

> *He who has an ear, let him hear what the Spirit says to the churches. To him who overcomes I will give to eat from the tree of life, which is in the midst of the Paradise of God.* (Revelation 2:7)

Two benefits of being an overcomer are (1) you will *"eat from the tree of life,"* and (2) you will be in the *"Paradise of God."*

There are no limits to what you can do with the help of God. When your earthly life is over, everything you will have struggled through and overcome will all be worthwhile. What we have in this life now is worthless compared with knowing Jesus Christ and spending eternity with Him.

You Will Be Spared from the Second Death

If a person is not an overcomer, he won't be so fortunate as to spend eternity with Jesus. Those who do not know Jesus Christ as their Lord will be cast into a lake of fire. This is known as the *"second death"* (Revelation 21:8). These unfortunate souls will face torment that was designed for fallen angels. (See Matthew 25:41–46; Revelation 19:20; 20:10, 14–15.) Overcomers will escape this second death and will have eternal life.

> *He who has an ear, let him hear what the Spirit says to the churches. He who overcomes shall not be hurt by the second death.* (Revelation 2:11)

You Will Receive Secret Rewards

Jesus has certain rewards for His followers that are hidden, and overcomers are entitled to understand these hidden secrets. Each overcomer will also receive a special stone with a new name known only to that person and Jesus. You will not be just another face in heaven. Jesus will have a special name for you alone.

> *He who has an ear, let him hear what the Spirit says to the churches. To him who overcomes I will give some of the hidden manna to eat. And I will give him a white stone, and on the stone a new name written which no one knows except him who receives it.* (Revelation 2:17)

You Will Have Power Over the Nations

Another reward to overcomers will be *"power over the nations"*:

And he who overcomes, and keeps My works until the end, to him I will give power over the nations. (Revelation 2:26)

Many people today crave worldly power, yet very few of them have had power over nations. As an over-comer, you will have this ability. Jesus, you, and other overcomers will rule and have more power and author-ity than any president, emperor, or king ever dreamed of having. (See also Revelation 5:10; 20:6; 22:5.)

Additional Blessings to Overcomers

Here are some additional promises to overcom-ers. Your name will be written in the Book of Life, and Jesus will announce you to His Father and the angels:

He who overcomes shall be clothed in white garments, and I will not blot out his name from the Book of Life; but I will confess his name before My Father and before His an-gels. (Revelation 3:5)

You will be given a prominent place in the tem-ple of God:

He who overcomes, I will make him a pillar in the temple of My God, and he shall go out no more. And I will write on him the name of My God and the name of the city of My God, the New Jerusalem, which comes down out of heaven from My God. And I will write on him My new name. (verse 12)

Jesus will share His throne with overcomers. We will sit in the throne room and seat of power for the universe:

> *To him who overcomes I will grant to sit with Me on My throne, as I also overcame and sat down with My Father on His throne.*
> (Revelation 3:21)

These promises are hard to imagine. We are indeed more than conquerors! We will be given honor and power.

All these things, however, are nothing compared with knowing and loving Jesus. We will all bow and worship Him, who is "*KING OF KINGS AND LORD OF LORDS*" (Revelation 19:16). He is worthy to be worshipped and to be given all honor, power, and glory forever.

MAKE THE MOST OF THE TIME YOU HAVE IN THIS LIFE, AND GLORIFY GOD IN EVERYTHING YOU DO.

Our time on this earth is minuscule when compared with the eternity we will spend with Jesus. In Jesus Christ, all Christians are overcomers. Being an overcomer is not an option. Make the most of the time you have in this life, and glorify God in everything you do.

The greater One lives within you, and you are triumphant in Him. The days of excuses are over; the days of limitation are over. Take your place as an overcomer. There are no limits in God. Therefore, go out and tell others the gospel of Jesus Christ. Go out and win the lost for Him. Go out and deliver the captives. Go out and set at liberty those who are oppressed. (See Luke 4:18.) You are an overcomer—"just do it"!

Chapter Twelve

Faith Is Victorious

Throughout this book, we have been exploring what it means to overcome limitations in our lives. In chapter 1, we looked at the Greek word for "*victory*" used in 1 John 5:4, which is *nike*.

> *For whatever is born of God overcomes the world. And this is the victory [nike] that has overcome the world; our faith.* (1 John 5:4)

You cannot remove limitations without faith. By faith, we overcome in Jesus Christ. By faith, we are made "*more than conquerors through* [Christ] *who loved us*" (Romans 8:37). There are no circumstances in which we can be defeated when we serve God in faith. We will experience trials of our faith, but, if we endure with patience, we will have victory. (See James 1:2–4.)

If you are going to remove all the limits that grieve God in your personal life, your spiritual life, your physical life, your mental life, and your emotional life, you must do so by faith. In the following two scriptural accounts, Jesus emphasized that we can have "mountain-moving" faith.

Mountain-Moving Faith

The Lesson of the Fig Tree

Mark 11 describes how Jesus entered Jerusalem riding on a donkey. This was a triumphant procession. Jesus was hailed as King of the Jews. People put palm branches on the road and cried out, *"Hosanna! 'Blessed is He who comes in the name of the Lord!'"* (Mark 11:9). It was a time of great rejoicing.

After being in Jerusalem that day, Jesus left to spend the night in Bethany, just outside the city gates. The next morning, He was hungry. On His way into the city again, He passed by a fig tree, hoping to find some figs for breakfast, but the tree had no fruit. Jesus said to the tree, *"Let no one eat fruit from you ever again"* (Mark 11:14). The disciples who were traveling with Him heard Him speak to this tree. Then, Jesus went on to clear the temple in Jerusalem of money changers, rebuking them for robbing the people. He finished His work for the day and went back to Bethany for the evening. (See verses 15–19.)

The next day, Jesus and His disciples passed by the fig tree that Jesus had cursed, and the disciples saw that it had withered from the roots. Peter remembered what Jesus had said to the tree and pointed it out to Him. Jesus used this example of speaking to a tree to teach His disciples about faith and prayer. He discussed how important it was to have faith in God, telling them that, if they had faith, they not only could speak to fig trees, but they could even speak to mountains and have them thrown into the sea.

So Jesus answered and said to them, "Have faith in God. For assuredly, I say to you,

*whoever says to this mountain, 'Be removed
and be cast into the sea,' and does not doubt
in his heart, but believes that those things
he says will be done, he will have whatever
he says. Therefore I say to you, whatever
things you ask when you pray, believe that
you receive them, and you will have them."*
(Mark 11:22–24)

You, too, can have mountain-moving faith to remove the limits from your life. The same principle is
demonstrated in the following account.

THE DELIVERANCE OF A TORMENTED YOUNG MAN

One day, a man whose son was suffering greatly from recurring seizures brought the young man
to Jesus' disciples. The disciples could do nothing
to help him. The father then took his son to Jesus.
Jesus rebuked His disciples for their lack of faith,
and then He cured the young man. Afterward, the
disciples asked Jesus why they had not been able to
help the man's son.

*Jesus said to them, "Because of your unbe-
lief; for assuredly, I say to you, if you have
faith as a mustard seed, you will say to this
mountain, 'Move from here to there,' and it
will move; and nothing will be impossible
for you."* (Matthew 17:20)

Jesus explained to them that they had failed
to heal the young man because of their unbelief. I
am sure it was hard for the disciples to accept the
fact that it was unbelief that had hindered them from

healing someone. Everyone likes to think he has great faith. Yet Jesus said it was their lack of faith that had limited them.

THE WORD OF GOD IS THE SEED OF FAITH THAT OVERCOMES LIMITS

> FAITH MAKES ALL THINGS POSSIBLE. IT IS A SUPERNATURAL FORCE THAT ALLOWED JESUS TO DO THE "IMPOSSIBLE."

Faith makes all things possible. It is a supernatural force that allowed Jesus to do the "impossible." Jesus compared mountain-moving faith to a tiny mustard seed. A seed has the power to grow and develop, when given the proper conditions. Seeds grow into plants or trees that produce fruit containing more seeds. In a similar way, faith grows and yields fruit when it is cultivated under the proper conditions. Jesus taught His disciples a parable, which we call the parable of the sower, that highlights this truth. (See Mark 4:3–32.)

To summarize this parable, a farmer went out and sowed seed. Some of the seed fell on the path and was eaten by birds. Other seed fell on rocky soil, and because it could not grow deep roots, it withered in the sun. Still other seed fell among thorns that grew alongside it and choked it, so that it could not produce fruit. But some seed fell on good ground and was fruitful.

Jesus explained this parable to His disciples and said that the farmer represented someone sowing the Word of God. The Word is the seed for faith.

Some people hear the Word and live lives of overcoming faith. Others hear the same Word and live lives of defeat.

The path represents those who hear the Word but allow it to go in one ear and out the other, because Satan comes immediately to steal it from them. When Satan steals the Word before it has time to grow, no fruit can be produced.

Others hear the Word and begin to act on it, but because they do not cultivate their faith and allow it to develop good roots, they never produce lasting fruit. (Compare John 15:16.) This is what happened with regard to the rocky soil. Jesus said people like this are easily offended when affliction or persecution attacks them. When you are not rooted and grounded in the Word of God, your faith will fail when life begins to heat up, because such trials come to steal the Word from us. We must be established in faith and love.

The people represented by thorny soil are those who hear the Word but, because they are filled with the cares of the world, fail to produce fruit. People can become distracted by a desire to acquire riches and material things. The desire to accumulate wealth is deceitful and often causes the seed of faith to be lost. Faith that overcomes the world cannot be cultivated in someone who is distracted by the things of the world. A person who has overcoming faith will not allow himself to be sidetracked by the cares of living. He knows God is his source for all good things, and he has faith that God will meet his needs.

The good soil represents people who have successful faith. They take the Word of God into their hearts and allow it to be rooted and established there so that it can produce fruit. Paul wrote, *"As you have therefore received Christ Jesus the Lord, so walk in Him, rooted and built up in Him and established in the faith, as you have been taught, abounding in it with thanksgiving"* (Colossians 2:6–7). Faith is the victory that overcomes the world. The Word of God is the seed of faith that causes you to triumph over limitations in your life. Jesus has won the victory, but you must live a life of faith to produce fruit for God.

CULTIVATING THE FRUIT OF FAITH

The apostle Paul listed faith as part of the fruit of the Holy Spirit:

> *But the fruit of the Spirit is love, joy, peace, longsuffering, kindness, goodness, faithfulness* [*"faith"* KJV], *gentleness, self-control. Against such there is no law.*
> (Galatians 5:22–23)

The Holy Spirit lives within every believer, and as a believer begins to act in faith on the Word of God, the fruit of the Spirit is produced in his or her life.

> FAITH IS PRODUCED IN THE LIFE OF A BELIEVER WHEN THE BELIEVER IS PART OF THE TREE, JESUS CHRIST.

Fruit is a natural product of trees that are healthy. Thriving trees do not have to struggle to produce fruit; they flower and bear fruit when the season is right. A tree produces fruit through its branches. Yet the branches cannot produce fruit by themselves. They depend on the rest of the tree—its trunk and roots—to supply them with nutrients and water. Likewise, faith is produced in the life of a believer when the believer is part of the Tree, Jesus Christ.

Jesus compared Himself to a grapevine and His followers to the branches:

> *I am the vine, you are the branches. He who abides in Me, and I in him, bears much fruit; for without Me you can do nothing. If anyone does not abide in Me, he is cast out as a branch and is withered; and they gather them and throw them into the fire, and they are burned. If you abide in Me, and My words abide in you, you will ask what you desire, and it shall be done for you. By this My Father is glorified, that you bear much fruit; so you will be My disciples.*
>
> (John 15:5–8)

Jesus illustrated how important the main part of the vine is to the branches. If we live attached to the Vine, we will be fruitful and productive. If we live detached from the Vine, we will become spiritually withered. Jesus said that withered branches are cut off and burned. Branches that are attached to the vine, however, remain alive and strong. Again, the branches have no power in themselves. They exist so that the fruit has a place to grow. Only branches that are well connected to the Vine will be fruitful.

GOD HAS GIVEN FAITH TO US ALL

Faith is not something that only a few people are entitled to have. God has given each of us a *"measure of faith."* Paul wrote,

> *For I say, through the grace given to me, to everyone who is among you, not to think of himself more highly than he ought to think, but to think soberly, as God has dealt to each one a measure of faith.*
>
> (Romans 12:3)

God has a measure of faith for everyone. He gives us the seed of the Word of God, and the Word produces faith in those who hear it and establish it in their hearts.

FAITH COMES BY HEARING THE WORD

> *So then faith comes by hearing, and hearing by the word of God.*   (Romans 10:17)

There are two Greek words that are translated into English as "*word*" in the New Testament: *rhema* and *logos*. *Rhema* is a declaration or command, while *logos* implies an idea or concept. Paul used *rhema* for "*word*" in the above verse. Let us look at a few additional verses where these words are used and discover the nuances of meaning that are often lost in translation.

A *RHEMA* WORD GIVES LIFE

The word *rhema* was used by New Testament writers in the following verses:

> *But [Jesus] answered and said, "It is written, 'Man shall not live by bread alone, but by every word [rhema] that proceeds from the mouth of God.'"*   (Matthew 4:4)

*If you abide in Me, and My words [rhema]
abide in you, you will ask what you desire,
and it shall be done for you.* (John 15:7)

*It is the Spirit who gives life; the flesh prof-
its nothing. The words [rhema] that I speak
to you are spirit, and they are life.*
(John 6:63)

Jesus said His *rhema* provides life itself. When God personally declares something to someone—in other words, when God gives a *rhema* word to someone—if that person receives it by faith, it will come to pass. For example, Mary did not doubt the word of God that came to her through the angel. She received it and became the mother of Jesus. (See Luke 1:26–38.)

> **WHEN GOD GIVES A *RHEMA* WORD TO SOMEONE, IF THAT PERSON RECEIVES IT BY FAITH, IT WILL COME TO PASS.**

When Jesus was hungry after having fasted in the wilderness for forty days, the devil tried to tempt Him to turn stones into bread. (See Matthew 4:1–3.) Jesus could have turned the stones into bread to satisfy His need for food. After all, He had turned water into wine; turning rocks into bread certainly would have been possible. However, He did not fall for the devil's trick and refused to act on the devil's words. Instead, He said He would act only on the *rhema* word from God. If Jesus did not hear God tell Him to turn the stones into bread, He would not do it.

Rhema, therefore, is the word that God speaks to a person's heart for a particular situation. God gives us His *rhema* to direct and guide our lives. *Rhema* is different from *logos*, the other Greek word we translate as "word."

A *Logos* Word Gives Information

Logos is the Greek term more often translated as "word" in the New Testament. It occurs 330 times, while *rhema* occurs only seventy times. *Logos* is most often found in the phrase *"word of the Lord"* (see, for example, Luke 22:61) or *"word of God"* (see, for example, Mark 7:13). For some additional examples, the word *logos* is used for *"word"* in the following verses:

> *In the beginning was the Word [logos], and the Word [logos] was with God, and the Word [logos] was God.* (John 1:1)

> *The sower sows the word [logos].* (Mark 4:14)

> *Making the word [logos] of God of no effect through your tradition which you have handed down.* (Mark 7:13)

Logos is the idea or concept of something said. A derivative of *logos* is *logikos*, the word from which the English word *logic* comes. *Logikos* is used for *"word"* in the following verse: *"As newborn babes, desire the pure milk of the word [logikos], that you may grow thereby"* (1 Peter 2:2).

The word *logos* can also mean "an account given for something."

So he called him and said to him, "What is this I hear about you? Give an account [logos] of your stewardship, for you can no longer be steward." (Luke 16:2)

In Revelation 12:11, "*the word of their testimony*" that overcomes the devil is the *logos*. When you give an account of what God has done for you, this word defeats the enemy.

And they overcame him by the blood of the Lamb and by the word [logos] of their testimony, and they did not love their lives to the death. (Revelation 12:11)

EXERCISING FAITH THROUGH *RHEMA* AND *LOGOS*

God's Word is both *rhema* and *logos*. You should desire to study the *logos* of the Bible and to renew your mind with the *logos* of God. However, faith comes by hearing the *rhema* of God. The *rhema* of God is necessary to live in victory over your limitations.

Faith begins when you hear the *rhema* of God in your heart. The Spirit of God lives in you, and as you become more familiar with the Bible, or the *logos* of God, the Word becomes alive in you. The Spirit of God activates the words of the Bible, and they become the revealed Word of

THE SPIRIT OF GOD ACTIVATES THE WORDS OF THE BIBLE, AND THEY BECOME THE REVEALED WORD OF GOD TO YOU.

God to you; they become the *rhema* that you must live by.

The *rhema* is the life of God that comes from the Vine and flows to the branches. The *rhema* of God is what will produce fruit in the branches. You can do nothing by yourself. It is the *rhema* of God that strengthens you and makes you able to do all things.

The *logos* says you are more than a conqueror. The *logos* says you are an overcomer. The *logos* says there are no limits to what you can ask God. However, it is the faith that comes from the *rhema* of God that allows you to be more than a conqueror and to triumph over your limits.

We must recognize the difference between acting on a personal command from God and acting presumptuously on our own. People can fall into trouble when they act on something they are not sure about. Peter had a *rhema* from God to walk on water when he saw Jesus walking on the sea.

> *Peter answered* [Jesus] *and said, "Lord, if it is You, command me to come to You on the water." So He said, "Come." And when Peter had come down out of the boat, he walked on the water to go to Jesus.*
>
> (Matthew 14:28–29)

Jesus told Peter to come out of the boat and onto the water. If you do not have a *rhema* from God, do not try this on your own; you will sink. Do not presume that because Jesus told Peter he could walk on the water, you can walk on water, too.

In another illustration, Jesus had a *rhema* from His Father to put mud on a blind man's eyes to heal him. (See John 9:6.) If you do not have a *rhema* from God to do this, it will not work. Peter had a *rhema* from God to command a lame man in the temple to rise and walk in the name of Jesus. (See Acts 3:6.) Miracles are made possible when you receive a *rhema* from God.

Jesus said,

> *If you abide in Me, and My words [rhema] abide in you, you will ask what you desire, and it shall be done for you.* (John 15:7)

When the *rhema* dwells in you, you can ask for whatever you need, and it will be done for you. To know God's *rhema*, you have to abide in Jesus. To know God's *rhema*, you have to be sanctified by the *logos*. To know God's *rhema*, you have to spend time with Him in prayer and in reading the Bible. Then, when you know you have God's *rhema*, you can shatter all limits! Nothing will be impossible when you hear the *rhema* of God and have faith to believe it will come to pass.

UPROOTING HINDRANCES TO FAITH

Faith is the key to removing limits. Therefore, in addition to building and exercising our faith through *rhema* and *logos*, we must be alert to those things that weaken our faith, or that prevent faith from becoming established in our lives, so that we can recognize and uproot them. The following are several limitations that threaten to undermine faith.

UNBELIEF

The opposite of faith is unbelief, and unbelief prevents many people from receiving God's blessings. Remember that all the Israelites were eligible to receive the blessing of the Promised Land. Yet, because of their unbelief, most of them did not live to receive it. (See Hebrews 3:17–19.) Just because you are eligible for blessings doesn't mean you have faith to receive them.

When Jesus visited His hometown of Nazareth, He was not accepted by the people, and He was unable to do many miracles there. Matthew clearly stated the reason why: "*So they were offended at Him. But Jesus said to them, 'A prophet is not without honor except in his own country and in his own house.' Now He did not do many mighty works there because of their **unbelief**"* (Matthew 13:57–58, emphasis added).

A passage from the book of Luke sheds a little more light on the situation.

> *Then* [Jesus] *said, "Assuredly, I say to you, no prophet is accepted in his own country. But I tell you truly, many widows were in Israel in the days of Elijah, when the heaven was shut up three years and six months, and there was a great famine throughout all the land; but to none of them was Elijah sent except to Zarephath, in the region of Sidon, to a woman who was a widow. And many lepers were in Israel in the time of Elisha the prophet, and none of them was cleansed except Naaman the Syrian." So all those in the synagogue, when they heard*

these things, were filled with wrath.
(Luke 4:24–28)

Jesus reminded the people in His hometown about how God had sent the prophets Elijah and Elisha to a woman and a man from countries outside Israel to bless them. God used the prophet Elijah to miraculously supply a Sidonian widow's need for food by multiplying the last little bit of flour and oil she had. (See 1 Kings 17:9–16.) God brought Naaman the Syrian leper to the prophet Elisha to receive healing from his leprosy. (See 2 Kings 5:1–14.) There were many citizens of Israel who needed miracles at that time, but God had to go outside the country to find people with the faith to receive them. When Jesus told His townsmen these things, they became angry with him.

Unbelief kept most of those in Nazareth from receiving healing or any other blessings. Jesus used the examples of the widow from Sidon and the leper from Syria to illustrate the people's unbelief and to reveal it to them. The widow and the leper had faith, and they received from God, but the folks in Jesus' hometown had unbelief and did not.

The situation is no different today. Many people are angry with God for not healing their sick bodies or blessing them financially. If you tell them it is because of their unbelief, they will become angry with you, too. Unbelief is a limitation in the lives of many Christians that keeps them from receiving the blessings of God.

Sickness, disease, and financial lack are problems we still face in the world every day. Faith in God

JESUS CAME TO TEACH US HOW TO RECEIVE WHAT WE NEED FROM GOD BY FAITH, AND HE DID NOT LIMIT IT TO SPIRITUAL NEEDS ALONE.

is the solution to overcoming these limitations in our lives. Jesus came to teach us how to receive what we need from God by faith, and He did not limit it to spiritual needs alone. God can meet your physical and financial needs, as well as your spiritual needs. He is willing to meet your physical and financial needs if you will overcome the limit of unbelief.

It is hard for many people to understand that unbelief is a limitation, that it keeps them from receiving God's blessings. Ask yourself this question: "Is it possible that Jesus cannot do many mighty works in our churches today because of unbelief?" The answer to this question is an emphatic "Yes!" Another good question to ask is this: "If we had faith, could Jesus do mighty works in our churches today?" The answer to this question is also an emphatic "Yes!"

DOUBT AND FEAR

Doubt and fear are also enemies that rob faith of its effectiveness.

> So Jesus answered and said to them, "Assuredly, I say to you, if you have faith and do not doubt, you will not only do what was done to the fig tree, but also if you say to this mountain, 'Be removed and be cast into the sea,' it will be done." (Matthew 21:21)

Doubt is different from unbelief. Unbelief is denying that the Word of God is true. Doubt acknowledges that the Word of God is true, but it fails to believe the Word is true now for a particular situation. Doubt says, "I am not sure the time is right. Maybe later, but not now." In contrast, faith is always in the present tense; it is something you have now. Faith says, "It is time to receive at this particular moment." Faith is being convinced that God's words are truer than the negative circumstances you are in. When the light of faith is in your heart, the darkness of both doubt and fear disappears, because doubt and fear go hand in hand. Fear is expecting that the worst will happen. Fear is not only a wrong way of thinking, but it is also a strong emotion.

> *And Peter answered* [Jesus] *and said, "Lord, if it is You, command me to come to You on the water." So He said, "Come." And when Peter had come down out of the boat, he walked on the water to go to Jesus. But when he saw that the wind was boisterous, he was afraid; and beginning to sink he cried out, saying, "Lord, save me!" And immediately Jesus stretched out His hand and caught him, and said to him, "O you of little faith, why did you doubt?"*
> (Matthew 14:28–31)

Peter saw Jesus walking on the water, and he wanted to walk on the water, too. Jesus commanded Peter to step out of the boat, which was a *rhema* word, as we discussed earlier, and Peter began to walk on the water. Yet, when he looked around and saw the wind and the waves, he started to fear for his safety. He then doubted, and so he sank. Jesus reached out and steadied him, and I imagine that all of Peter's fear and doubt quickly disappeared.

Fear and doubt limit you from receiving from God. Even though Peter had a *rhema* word from the Lord to walk on top of the sea, he began to sink because of his fear and doubt. Fear and doubt keep us from believing the *rhema* words we hear from the Lord. However, with the help of Jesus, we can do mighty works.

> ## MANY OF US ARE SO PROGRAMMED TO IMAGINE THE WORST WILL HAPPEN THAT WE MISS OUT ON MANY MIRACLES.

Many of us are so programmed to imagine that the worst will happen that we miss out on many miracles. God wants us to learn to overcome our fears and doubts. He wants us to be people of great faith. Fear and doubt keep our faith small, and God wants us to have unlimited faith. If we have faith instead of doubt and fear, we can move mountains. Victorious faith overcomes the limits of unbelief, doubt, and fear.

LACK OF ACTION

Third, a lack of action will limit the effectiveness of our faith, because faith requires corresponding actions. Faith is more than just talking. Faith is both talking *and* doing.

> *For as the body without the spirit is dead, so faith without works is dead also.*
>
> (James 2:26)

Years ago, a man and his wife attended a meeting I held, and the wife made her husband come up to the altar with her for prayer. When I inquired what they wanted prayer for, the wife told me that she was upset with her husband because he would not work. She was working and paying all the bills for their household. He said he was living by faith. So, I asked him to tell me more about the situation, and he said the Lord had told him to start a ministry. When I asked if he had started it, he said he had not. It turns out he was not doing anything to prepare for the ministry. He was just sitting around the house watching TV and doing nothing productive.

I looked at the wife and told her to quit feeding him. If she would stop cooking for him, he would go to work. I told the husband that the Bible says, "If you do not work, you do not eat." (See 2 Thessalonians 3:10.) He did not like what I said, and he left angry.

This man was not living in faith because he had no corresponding actions to go along with his words. He said he was going to start a ministry, yet he was not doing anything but being lazy. Faith without works is a dead faith. If you do not add actions to your faith, you are limited from being blessed by God.

LIVING BY FAITH PLEASES GOD

God takes pleasure in those who have faith and act on His promises. He is not pleased with those who lack faith.

> *Now the just shall live by faith; but if anyone draws back, My soul has no pleasure in him.* (Hebrews 10:38)

God is pleased when you use your faith to break limits in your life. He rewards you for seeking Him and doing His will.

> *But without faith it is impossible to please Him, for he who comes to God must believe that He is, and that He is a rewarder of those who diligently seek Him.*
>
> (Hebrews 11:6)

The writer of the book of Hebrews continued in the next few verses of chapter 11 to talk about the faith, obedience, and actions of heroes of the Bible. All these people overcame the limitations of the world. By faith, Noah built an ark and saved the human race from extinction. (See verse 7.) By faith, Abraham left his home country and received many blessings from God. (See verses 8–10.) By faith, Abraham's wife, Sarah, conceived and had a child, who was a direct ancestor of Jesus. (See verses 11–12.) Each of these triumphs resulted from the individual's faith in God. Reading about the faith of these heroes helps us to understand that whoever is born of God overcomes the limitations of the world, *"and this is the victory that has overcome the world; our faith"* (1 John 5:4).

CHAPTER THIRTEEN

INCREASE BEYOND YOUR LIMITS

With the help of Christ, you can do all things.

> *I can do all things through Christ who strengthens me.* (Philippians 4:13)

Being able to do "*all things*" means nothing can hinder you. Even though you are weak in yourself, when you live by faith in the power of God, there is no limit to what you can do in Christ.

God has a wonderful plan for your life. He loves you and wants you to return that love to Him. When you love God, you show your love by your actions, and there is more power inside the least Christian than you could ever imagine. There is no excuse for you not to glorify God with your life!

You can throw off the limitations that are keeping you from being all God wants you to be. Whatever state you are in spiritually, financially, emotionally, or physically, you can overcome your limits with His help. As we have seen, *Unleashing Heaven's Blessings* is about entering into the fullness of God. The

Lord has an unlimited plan for you, and when you find His will for your life, you can reach beyond your current circumstances and tap into His limitless resources. No more limitations means you are able to do all things through Christ who strengthens you. No more limitations means receiving the richness of God's provision.

If you have been honest with yourself as you've been reading this book, you have realized that there are some areas in your life in which you have set limits where God is concerned. You have set boundaries for various reasons. If you will allow the Holy Spirit to reveal these limits to you, He will. God wants you to recognize your limitations so you can go beyond them.

ESTABLISHING NEW PARAMETERS

God spoke to the Israelites about how He planned to enlarge the boundaries of their nation.

> *For I will cast out the nations before you and enlarge your borders; neither will any man covet your land when you go up to appear before the* LORD *your God three times in the year.* (Exodus 34:24)

The Lord was talking about defeating the enemies of the nation of Israel, and the principle at work there applies to us, too. He said He was going to cast out those nations, or those obstacles, before them and enlarge their borders.

God promised the Israelites that if they followed His words, He would increase them beyond their limits. If you have faith in God's words, He will remove the obstacles before you. He wants to extend your boundaries. God will give you the ability to do more than you ever thought possible. The seed of faith in your heart will grow, and you will steadily increase beyond your limitations.

> GOD WILL GIVE YOU THE ABILITY TO DO MORE THAN YOU EVER THOUGHT POSSIBLE.

In this chapter, we are going to look at three ways by which you can increase. First, you can increase by setting specific goals. Goals help you to reach past your old limits and establish new parameters. Second, you can increase by speaking words of faith. The words you say either reinforce your old limits, or they help you to expand to new horizons. Third, you can increase by taking action. Actions determine how far you will go with the goals you set and the words you say. These three areas are vital for helping you to apply your faith to real-life situations.

1. INCREASE BY SETTING GOALS

If you do not know where you are going, how are you to know if or when you have reached your destination? Clearly, goals are essential, and we should set them for ourselves, especially for our spiritual lives. The most important goal for Christians to pursue is our calling in God. The apostle Paul said,

> *I press toward the goal for the prize of the upward call of God in Christ Jesus.*
> (Philippians 3:14)

Paul set his sights on a marker that was farther ahead than where he was at the time, and he moved toward it with great focus and determination. Your primary goal should be to know Jesus Christ and to fulfill His plan for your life.

SET GOALS TO DEVELOP YOUR SPIRITUAL LIFE

Have you ever been praying, and all of a sudden you feel as if your prayer is not going any higher than the ceiling? You do not feel like you are getting through to God. Then, are there other times when you are praying, and you think you are really making contact with heaven? That is when you know you are in His presence. You should want to enter into His presence every time you pray.

If you are limited in your prayer life, you are going to be limited in your results. This is why you need to set goals for your spiritual life. If you already know how to set goals for your business or your family, you can apply some of the same methods. The most important things you can do to help develop your spiritual life are to pray consistently and read your Bible daily. Set goals to spend time in prayer and Bible study, and follow through with them, and God will give you wisdom to know His will for your life.

You can set goals for whatever you want to do for God, including serving in and through your local church. God will show you what to do to please Him, and He will guide you in the right steps to take.

You may be able to make many plans, but the plan that will work best is the one that has the Lord's blessing. When you find His plan and follow it, you will be assured of success.

Trust in the LORD with all your heart, and lean not on your own understanding; in all your ways acknowledge Him, and He shall direct your paths.   (Proverbs 3:5–6)

With the help of God, you can set a goal to overcome any limitation in your life. Do you have a problem with unforgiveness, anger, or pride? Set a goal to overcome it. Do you have a problem with foul language? Set a goal to overcome it. Do you lack joy in your life? Are you dry spiritually? Set goals to find joy and be watered spiritually.

> WITH THE HELP OF GOD, YOU CAN SET A GOAL TO OVERCOME ANY LIMITATION IN YOUR LIFE.

You may need to make some significant changes in your life to accomplish your major goals. So, after setting the major goals, develop smaller goals that will enable you to make these significant changes. Goals help you move in the direction you need to go, and they assist you to make the necessary corrections to stay on the right course.

If you are diligent in seeking God's will for your life, you will find it. And if you set specific goals, you can move toward fulfilling that will. When you are obedient to God's word to you, you will be successful, and you will fulfill His plan.

SET GOALS TO DEVELOP YOUR FINANCIAL LIFE

Goals are necessary not only for spiritual matters, but also for other areas in life. For instance, most people do not make adequate financial plans for their retirement. They work for years, and when they retire, they have nothing to show for it. Unfortunately, too many people end up depending on someone else to support them during their golden years. Without any extra money besides government checks, many people live out their retirement years in a severely limited way.

The Bible tells us that even ants plan for their future. How much more should human beings, God's most precious creation, plan for their futures?

> *Go to the ant, you sluggard! Consider her ways and be wise, which, having no captain, overseer or ruler, provides her supplies in the summer, and gathers her food in the harvest. How long will you slumber, O sluggard? When will you rise from your sleep? A little sleep, a little slumber, a little folding of the hands to sleep; so shall your poverty come on you like a prowler, and your need like an armed man.* (Proverbs 6:6–11)

To develop your financial life, you should ask yourself these questions: Where do I want to be twenty years from now? What kind of nest egg do I want to have saved by the time I retire from my job? What kind of method or plan do I need to implement in order to accomplish my retirement goals? What amount do I want to have saved by the time I am sixty-five?

The best time to start saving for your retirement is when you are young, early in your working career. The longer you wait, the greater the amounts of money you will need to put into your savings to obtain your goals. And the older you become, the less time you will have to properly save money. If you can figure out on your own what amount of money you need for retirement, and if you can save toward this goal, that is great. But if you cannot, you need to consult a professional to help you make a financial plan for your future.

Then, whatever you want to accomplish for your retirement is your goal. You should set aside a certain amount of money each month now in order to be able to fulfill your goal in later years. It may not seem like much, but it will add up to a lot if you do it consistently, year after year.

Make Your Goals Measurable and Realistic

Keep in mind that goals should be measurable and realistic. To assure these results, break each goal down into parts. Setting a goal "to make more money" or "to lose some weight" is not specific enough. You need to set a goal to make a certain amount of money, or to lose a certain amount of weight, in a certain amount of time.

For example, if you are one hundred pounds overweight, do not attempt to lose a hundred pounds in one month. Try to lose two pounds a week. Change your eating habits and your lifestyle. That approach will bring about long-term changes.

> AFTER YOU SET A GOAL, YOU SHOULD TAKE SOME ACTION IMMEDIATELY.

After you set a goal, you should take some action

immediately. Just as you wouldn't wait until all the traffic lights along the roadways to your destination were green before getting in your car and driving toward it, you should start where you are today to take steps toward a new future. It is often helpful to learn new skills and knowledge to help you meet your goals.

LEARN TO PRIORITIZE YOUR DAYS

Setting goals makes it easier for you to order the priorities in your life. By having clearly defined goals, you can make decisions about how you will spend your time. Every day, you should review your goals and recommit to work toward them.

Everyone is in a different place in life and will therefore need to establish or reinforce priorities in relation to his or her specific needs. I have learned to prioritize my time, even though I am still learning how to use my time wisely. I have had to learn to prioritize my goals and projects. If we are not careful, we can lose a whole day and not accomplish important tasks because of distractions. It is Satan's job to distract us from doing the will of the Lord.

Time is one of the most precious commodities we have. Once a day is over, we can never have those twenty-four hours back. You should make the most of each day.

> *See then that you walk circumspectly, not as fools but as wise, redeeming the time, because the days are evil. Therefore do not be unwise, but understand what the will of the Lord is.* (Ephesians 5:15–17)

Here is one method you can use to set priorities for what you need to accomplish each day. I carry a daily planner, and I assign priorities to the things I need to complete. If I have ten things I want to do, I will assign one of three priority designations to each of them: A, B, or C. "A" is my top priority; I must do it today. "B" is important and needs to be done, but it is not the most urgent priority; it can be done the next day, if necessary. "C" is something that should be done but can be done later if I do not finish all the As and Bs today.

This system works well for doing the work of the ministry, and it can be applied to other situations, as well. If you are a homemaker, a businessperson, a student, or anyone else, you can use the A, B, C system to set priorities and plan your daily activities.

How will you know when you have accomplished anything if you do not set goals? Setting up a mark in the distance, or in the future, helps you to measure progress toward a particular goal. And setting goals helps you to know when you have completed what you started out to do.

Goals and priorities do involve taking risks. You risk failure whenever you set a goal. Yet every risk also carries with it a potential reward. The greatest risks usually return the greatest rewards. Goals will help you determine what risks you want to take.

2. Increase by the Words You Speak

The second important aspect of establishing new parameters for your life is to change the way you speak. Consider for a moment the significance of words.

GOD CREATED EVERYTHING BY SPEAKING WORDS

When God created the world, He first spoke words. The creation account in Genesis is full of statements that demonstrate the power of His words. Every day, whatever God said came to pass. He created the land and seas by first speaking words. He created plants, animals, and human beings by speaking words. (See Genesis 1:3–27.) You and I are here today because He spoke words that came to pass. In the book of Isaiah, God indicates that every word He speaks is valuable and accomplishes something significant.

> *For as the rain comes down, and the snow from heaven, and do not return there, but water the earth, and make it bring forth and bud, that it may give seed to the sower and bread to the eater, so shall My word be that goes forth from My mouth; it shall not return to Me void, but it shall accomplish what I please, and it shall prosper in the thing for which I sent it.* (Isaiah 55:10–11)

GOD MADE HUMAN BEINGS IN HIS IMAGE AND GAVE THEM THE ABILITY TO CREATE WITH WORDS.

God made human beings in His image and gave them the ability to speak and to create with words, too. Your tongue is a small part of your body, but it can bring either much damage or much blessing. (See James 3:5–6; Proverbs 13:2.) Jesus said, *"For by your words you will be justified, and by your words you will be condemned"* (Matthew 12:37). He also said that His words are *"spirit"* and *"life"* (John 6:63). Your words can be spirit and life, as well. When you speak the words and language of God, you will increase beyond your limits and move into new areas.

God Created Language

God gave us the wonderful gift of communication through language. Words are carriers of meaning and an essential part of life. Without words, life as we know it would be impossible. Words allow us to talk to one another and to work together.

The fact that we have different languages in the world is the result of a miraculous act of God. At one time, everyone on earth spoke the same language. (See Genesis 11:1.) This reality enabled sinful men to work together for the wrong reasons, however. God had instructed human beings to expand beyond the limits of where they were living, but they were not willing to do so. Therefore, He caused them to speak in different languages, so that the various language groups would need to go and settle in their own areas of the world.

> *And they said, "Come, let us build ourselves a city, and a tower whose top is in the heavens; let us make a name for ourselves, lest we be scattered abroad over the face of the whole earth." But the Lord came down to see the city and the tower which the sons of men had built. And the Lord said, "Indeed the people are one and they all have one language, and this is what they begin to do; now nothing that they propose to do will be*

> *withheld from them. Come, let Us go down*
> *and there confuse their language, that they*
> *may not understand one another's speech."*
> *So the LORD scattered them abroad from*
> *there over the face of all the earth, and they*
> *ceased building the city. Therefore its name*
> *is called Babel, because there the LORD con-*
> *fused the language of all the earth; and*
> *from there the LORD scattered them abroad*
> *over the face of all the earth.*
> (Genesis 11:4–9)

God had to change their words to cause them to expand beyond their limits. He had to change their language to keep them from doing what they had planned to do. In Genesis 11:6, He said, *"Nothing that they propose to do will be withheld from them."* In other words, they could do whatever they wanted to do. Those ancient men were not building the Tower of Babel to glorify God. They were building it to make a name for themselves. God changed their language and their plans to suit His purpose. When God changed their words, He changed the way they lived.

GOD GAVE US LANGUAGE TO SPREAD THE GOSPEL

Thousands of years later, God again used different languages to change people. After Jesus' resurrection, He told His disciples to remain in Jerusalem until they received power from God to be His witnesses. (See Acts 1:8.) With this power came a supernatural gift of languages that enabled them to communicate with people from all over the world. This was the reverse of what had happened at the

Tower of Babel. God wanted Jesus' disciples to be understood by everyone in the world.

> *When the Day of Pentecost had fully come, they were all with one accord in one place. And suddenly there came a sound from heaven, as of a rushing mighty wind, and it filled the whole house where they were sitting. Then there appeared to them divided tongues, as of fire, and one sat upon each of them. And they were all filled with the Holy Spirit and began to speak with other tongues, as the Spirit gave them utterance. And there were dwelling in Jerusalem Jews, devout men, from every nation under heaven. And when this sound occurred, the multitude came together, and were confused, because everyone heard them speak in his own language. Then they were all amazed and marveled, saying to one another, "Look, are not all these who speak Galileans? And how is it that we hear, each in our own language in which we were born?"*
>
> (Acts 2:1–8)

On the Jewish day of Pentecost, people had come to Jerusalem from all over the world. The disciples spoke in *"other tongues,"* and all the people heard the good news of Jesus preached to them in their native languages.

This was the birthday of the church. When God gave the gift of speaking in unknown languages to the disciples, He changed the way they thought of themselves. They received supernatural power to be His witnesses throughout the world. When God changed the words they spoke, He changed the way they lived.

Today, the Bible is translated into more languages than any other book that has been written. Bible translators are still working hard to make the Word of God available to all language groups in the world. Billions of people are now able to read and understand the Word of God in their own native tongues, thanks to the work of thousands of dedicated missionaries who translated the Bible. The ability to have the words of God available to us in our native languages is a wonderful gift from Him.

WORDS SUPPORT YOUR FAITH

The words of God are powerful, and your words can be powerful, as well, in removing obstacles from your life. One of the most solid obstacles in the world is a mountain. Mountains seem impossible to move, yet Jesus saw nothing as impossible. Remember, He said that if we have faith, we can speak to a mountain, and it will be moved. You must learn how to speak to your limitations in faith, according to God's words.

> *For assuredly, I say to you, whoever says to this mountain, "Be removed and be cast into the sea," and does not doubt in his heart, but believes that those things he says will be done, he will have whatever he says.*
> (Mark 11:23)

Jesus emphasized *speaking* to the mountain. He mentioned speaking three times in this verse: (1) *"whoever says to this mountain..."*; (2) *"but believes that those things he says will be done..."*; (3) *"he will have whatever he says."* Jesus intertwined faith with speaking to the mountain; He pointed out that speaking to the mountain was an important part of having faith. Speaking words and having faith go hand in hand. You cannot have faith without speaking words of faith because words support your faith.

WORDS COME FROM YOUR HEART

Jesus also emphasized that what is in your heart comes out in the words you speak. What you say is what you believe.

> *A good man out of the good treasure of his heart brings forth good; and an evil man out of the evil treasure of his heart brings forth evil. For out of the abundance of the heart his mouth speaks.* (Luke 6:45)

You can change the way you live by changing what you say, and changing what you say starts with putting God's Word within your heart. Faith comes when you hear God speak to you. (See Romans 10:17.) The revelation of the Word of God to your heart

> **YOU CAN CHANGE THE WAY YOU LIVE BY CHANGING WHAT YOU SAY.**

causes you to speak faith-filled words, and these faith-filled words set spiritual forces into operation.

We experienced this truth when we were born again, because a faith-filled confession of the Lord Jesus brings salvation.

> *If you confess with your mouth the Lord Jesus and believe in your heart that God*

has raised Him from the dead, you will be
saved. For with the heart one believes unto
righteousness, and with the mouth confes-
sion is made unto salvation.

(Romans 10:9–10)

Your confession of Jesus as Lord of your life changed your eternal destiny. You will live with Jesus forever and escape the fires of hell because of the words you spoke in faith. The value of your words is priceless.

SPEAK TO YOUR LIMITATIONS

If you know God's will for you, and if you have faith in Him, you can speak to limiting "mountains" in your life and tell them to be "thrown into the sea," and they will be removed.

Note how Jesus spoke to situations and circumstances and changed them. He spoke to a storm and calmed it. (See Mark 4:39.) He spoke to a man who had been dead for four days, and he came back to life. (See John 11:39–44.) He spoke to people facing all kinds of adversities, and His words brought victory and triumph. After Jesus spoke and instructed His disciples, His words and teachings changed the world forever. Follow Jesus Christ's example. Learn to speak the words of God in faith, and you will smash through your limits.

- When financial lack tries to worry you, say, "My God supplies all my needs according to His riches in glory!" (See Philippians 4:19.) Begin to confess that you have abundance; confess that you have given, and that it shall be given to you. (See Luke 6:38.) Of course, you have to have planted a financial seed for God to multiply your harvest. Likewise, the Bible says the weak can say "*I am strong*" (Joel 3:10), and the poor can say "I am rich," through the grace of Christ. (See 2 Corinthians 8:9.)

- When sickness tries to overcome you, say, "I am healed by the stripes of Jesus!" (See 1 Peter 2:24.) It will do no good to reaffirm your sickness by saying you are sick; you already know that. What you desire is healing, and you have God's word that you will receive it.

- When fear of disaster tries to unsettle you, say, "God has not given me a spirit of fear. He has given me His love, power, and a sound mind!" (See 2 Timothy 1:7.)

How do you sow a seed of faith in your life? By saying what you desire, by speaking the Word of God. That's what Jesus did. Everything He did or said was to demonstrate the principles of the kingdom of heaven.

Please don't misunderstand. Just saying a bunch of words is not a magical formula for success. However, speaking the Word of God is part of operating in the principles of the kingdom. If Jesus' words live in us, we can speak His words back to God, and God will give us whatever we ask. (See John 15:7.) Recognize how valuable your words are. Remember that "*death and life are in the power of the tongue*" (Proverbs 18:21).

3. Increase by Taking Decisive Action

You can increase beyond your boundaries by the goals you set, by the words you speak, and by the actions you take. As we discussed in chapter 12, faith requires corresponding actions to be a living faith. Faith without actions is a dead faith.

> *Thus also faith by itself, if it does not have works, is dead. But someone will say, "You have faith, and I have works." Show me your faith without your works, and I will show you my faith by my works. You believe that there is one God. You do well. Even the demons believe; and tremble! But do you want to know, O foolish man, that faith without works is dead?* (James 2:17–20)

Just because you believe there is a God does not mean you have done much. The devil and his cohorts believe there is a God, too. You have to do more than have faith that God is real. You have to put your faith into action.

I believed that Jesus Christ was the Son of God while I was growing up and as a young adult. That was what I was told. I knew it as a fact, but I did not act on it until I was almost thirty years old. One day, while attending a church service, I acted in faith after I heard the pastor preach the Word of God and tell me I had to confess Jesus as my Lord and believe that God had raised Him from the dead. I walked down the aisle of the church, and when I stood in front of the preacher and confessed these truths with my mouth, I became born again. I was saved. After

I acted on the Word of God, I received a new life in Jesus Christ.

It is a beautiful thing to watch people understand the concept of unleashing heaven's blessings, with no more limitations, and put it into practice in their lives. People who put God's principles into action will see results. People who merely think about it briefly will never experience the fullness of God in their lives. The idea of no more limits will work in your life only if you take action.

> PEOPLE WHO PUT GOD'S PRINCIPLES INTO ACTION WILL SEE RESULTS.

You must do something. You have to take advantage of the opportunities God sends you. Do not miss those opportunities because of a lack of response. Put your faith into action.

FOLLOW DAVID'S EXAMPLE OF FAITH

In this chapter, we have examined three things that will help you go beyond your limitations: (1) increase by setting goals, (2) increase by the words you speak, and (3) increase by taking decisive action. In chapter 2, we talked about how David, a shepherd boy, triumphed over Goliath, a soldier and a giant of a man. David put his faith into action using the principles we have just been discussing. First, he set a goal to kill the giant. Second, he told the giant what he was going to do to him. Third, he did what he said he would do. Let us look more closely at these principles at work in David's triumph over Goliath.

DAVID SET A GOAL TO KILL THE GIANT

David set a goal to kill Goliath, so he analyzed his circumstances. He assessed his risks and rewards. He asked questions and found out that the man who succeeded in killing Goliath would receive financial rewards, freedom from taxes, and the hand of the king's daughter in marriage. David knew what the rewards would be when he accomplished his goal.

> *And all the men of Israel, when they saw [Goliath], fled from him and were dreadfully afraid. So the men of Israel said, "Have you seen this man who has come up? Surely he has come up to defy Israel; and it shall be that the man who kills him the king will enrich with great riches, will give him his daughter, and give his father's house exemption from taxes in Israel." Then David spoke to the men who stood by him, saying, "What shall be done for the man who kills this Philistine and takes away the reproach from Israel? For who is this uncircumcised Philistine, that he should defy the armies of the living God?" And the people answered him in this manner, saying, "So shall it be done for the man who kills him."*
>
> (1 Samuel 17:24–27)

King Saul tried to give David his own armor and sword with which to fight Goliath, but David did not take them because they were bulky, and because he had not proved them in battle. (See verses 38–39.) David developed a workable plan. He did know how to use his staff and sling as effective weapons, because shepherds had to use these implements to defend their flocks, so he prepared for battle by taking weapons he knew how to use. He took with him his staff, his slingshot, and five smooth stones.

> *Then he took his staff in his hand; and he chose for himself five smooth stones from the brook, and put them in a shepherd's bag, in a pouch which he had, and his sling was in his hand. And he drew near to the Philistine. So the Philistine came, and began drawing near to David, and the man who bore the shield went before him. And when the Philistine looked about and saw David, he disdained him; for he was only a youth, ruddy and good-looking. So the Philistine said to David, "Am I a dog, that you come to me with sticks?" And the Philistine cursed David by his gods. And the Philistine said to David, "Come to me, and I will give your flesh to the birds of the air and the beasts of the field!"* (1 Samuel 17:40–44)

DAVID SPOKE TO THE GIANT

David responded to the giant's threat by telling him he was going to kill him. This was no idle warning; David was experienced. He had already killed a lion and a bear while protecting his family's sheep. (See 1 Samuel 17:34–37.) David knew that he was in covenant with God, and he knew that the giant, an uncircumcised Philistine, was not in covenant with God. So, he spoke faith-filled words. He knew God was able to help him defeat his enemies, so he could boldly declare that he was going to kill Goliath.

Then David said to the Philistine, "You come to me with a sword, with a spear, and with a javelin. But I come to you in the name of the LORD of hosts, the God of the armies of Israel, whom you have defied. This day the LORD will deliver you into my hand, and I will strike you and take your head from you. And this day I will give the carcasses of the camp of the Philistines to the birds of the air and the wild beasts of the earth, that all the earth may know that there is a God in Israel. Then all this assembly shall know that the LORD does not save with sword and spear; for the battle is the LORD's, and He will give you into our hands."

(1 Samuel 17:45–47)

DAVID PUT HIS FAITH INTO ACTION

David did more than prepare to do battle and talk about it; he took immediate and decisive action. He followed through with his plan, putting his faith into motion.

So it was, when the Philistine arose and came and drew near to meet David, that David hastened and ran toward the army to meet the Philistine. Then David put his hand in his bag and took out a stone; and he slung it and struck the Philistine in his forehead, so that the stone sank into his forehead, and he fell on his face to the earth. So David prevailed over the Philistine with a sling and a stone, and struck the Philistine and killed him. But there was no sword in the hand of David. Therefore David ran and stood over the Philistine, took his sword and drew it out of its sheath and killed him, and cut off his head with it. And when the Philistines saw that their champion was dead, they fled. (1 Samuel 17:48–51)

Again, David believed God was going to help him, so he put his faith into action. The Bible says he *"hastened."* In other words, David was in a hurry to take out the giant. He ran toward Goliath and slung one of the stones, hitting him right between the eyes and knocking him out. He then took the giant's sword from him and cut off his head. David carried the giant's head around in triumph. The men of Israel were encouraged by David's feat, and they went on to win a great victory over the Philistine army. (See 1 Samuel 17:52–54.)

When God helped David to accomplish his goal, it brought great glory to Him. If a teenager like David can triumph over his enemy, you can triumph over your problems and circumstances. No matter how young or old you are, with the help of God, all things are possible for those who believe. (See, for example, Mark 9:23.)

> **IF A TEENAGER LIKE DAVID CAN TRIUMPH OVER HIS ENEMY, YOU CAN TRIUMPH OVER YOUR PROBLEMS.**

PUT YOUR FAITH INTO ACTION

You can put your goals into action, just as David did. The principles in this chapter will work for you in any aspect of your life: improving your marriage, making financial investments, increasing the scope of your ministry, and so forth. You can set goals, speak to your circumstances, and take decisive action.

Follow through with your goals. Follow through with your words. God rewards those who put their faith into motion. Faith with action is a live, vital faith. Faith with action moves mountains and slays giants. Faith with action causes you to triumph and to give glory to God.

CHAPTER FOURTEEN

OVERCOMING LIMITS DAILY

When I was in school at Henderson State College in Arkansas, I was not a Christian. I was lost, just like most of the other students were. On Friday nights, whenever we could, we would drive a few miles over to Hot Springs. One time, we went to a pizza parlor. The restaurant had a sign that read, "Free Beer Tomorrow!" When we saw that sign, we decided we were going to come back to this place tomorrow and drink free beer. So, the next day, we drove back to the pizza parlor, went in, and said, "We want our free beer." The owner looked at us, pointed at the sign, laughed, and said, "It's tomorrow!"

We were college students, and we thought we were so smart, but we learned a valuable lesson that night. Today is always today, and tomorrow is always the next day. Tomorrow never comes. When you wake up tomorrow, it is not going to be tomorrow; it is going to be today.

"TOMORROW" NEVER COMES, SO REJOICE IN THE "TODAY" THE LORD HAS MADE

Life comes one day at a time. Forget the past. Do not worry about tomorrow. Live your life one day at a time, and realize that God is with you every day.

The point is that living a life of faith is a daily exercise. Faith is not found in the future. Faith is not found in the past. Faith is always now. Faith is always in the present tense.

> *Now faith is the substance of things hoped for, the evidence of things not seen.*
>   (Hebrews 11:1)

Faith is an invisible force that directs your life every day. Today, God is working with you. Today, God is blessing you. Today, God is causing you to be an overcomer. Today, God is enabling you to be triumphant in Christ. Today, God wants you to live and enjoy your life. Today is the day the Lord has made. Rejoice in the day He has given you and be glad. (See Psalm 118:24.)

Everything You Do in Life Is Daily

You have to take action every day to remove the limitations from your life.

Life is a process. You have to take action every day to remove the limitations from your life. Do not wait for a crisis to overtake you. You should not wait until the furniture company backs a truck up to your door and repossesses your furniture to take action. You should not wait until the doctor says you have six months to live to take action. You should not wait months or years to forgive a person who has you all bent out of shape. You have to remove the limitations in your life starting today, right now.

Realize that much of what you must do in life has to be done daily. You were created with daily needs, such as food and sleep. Remember that God Himself worked on a daily basis when He created the world. (See Genesis 1.)

If you want to increase your physical capacity, for example, you need to exercise every day. If you start exercising daily, it may take you six months or a year to see results. You might be tempted to quit before you reach your goal. Yet, if you do not work at it every day, you will not succeed. Exercising once a month is not going to accomplish the results you are seeking.

The same principle applies to your spiritual vigor and growth. To be strong and filled with faith to remove limitations from your life, you must continually strengthen your spiritual muscles. In the previous chapter, we discussed making goals for our spiritual lives and taking action on them. The following are some guidelines for and insights into daily spiritual exercise that will help you to achieve those goals.

Give Us This Day Our Daily Bread

Pray Daily

In the Lord's Prayer, Jesus taught His disciples to pray for their bread every day: *"Give us this day our daily bread"* (Matthew 6:11). Bread can signify more than food. It can represent all the daily needs in your life. Bread also represents Jesus, because He referred to Himself as the *"bread of life"* (John 6:35).

It should be as important to you to pray on a daily basis as it is for you to eat. If you eat every day, you should also pray every day; you need to enter into the presence of God consistently through prayer. (See Psalm 140:13.)

The key to success in anything is to discipline yourself to do daily tasks related to your goals. Daily discipline is what sets champions apart from most other people. Whether or not you pray on a daily basis will determine how effective you will be as an overcomer and a champion in Christ. Praying every day is an important part of overcoming limits in your life.

READ AND STUDY YOUR BIBLE DAILY

Champions in Christ also need to read and study the Word of God on a daily basis. As you take God's Word into your spirit, it provides fuel for spiritual power, just as food provides fuel for your physical body.

Psalm 1 expresses the impact that daily Bible reading and study will have on your life. You should not delight in listening to ungodly counsel or to people with negative attitudes. Instead, you should delight in the Word of God.

> *Blessed is the man who walks not in the counsel of the ungodly, nor stands in the path of sinners, nor sits in the seat of the scornful; but his delight is in the law of the LORD, and in His law he meditates day and night. He shall be like a tree planted by the*

rivers of water, that brings forth its fruit in its season, whose leaf also shall not wither; and whatever he does shall prosper.

(Psalm 1:1–3)

Having daily devotions will feed and develop you spiritually. Seeds from fruit trees take years to grow into trees. In the same way, it takes years to become a mature Christian. After a fruit tree matures, it produces fruit. Spiritual growth will also produce fruit in its season. The key to spiritual growth is to nourish yourself daily with the Word to provide the necessary nutrients for growth.

Joshua became the leader of the nation of Israel after Moses died, and God used Joshua to take the Israelites from the desert, where they had wandered for forty years, into their Promised Land. The Promised Land was full of enemies, so Joshua had to lead the Israelites through many battles. He would not have been successful in achieving victory if he had not stayed connected to God daily. Moses had written the first five books of the Bible and left them with the Israelites, and God told Joshua to read these books.

This Book of the Law shall not depart from your mouth, but you shall meditate in it day and night, that you may observe to do according to all that is written in it. For then you will make your way prosperous, and then you will have good success.

(Joshua 1:8)

The Lord instructed Joshua to meditate on the Bible. To meditate does not mean to read quickly. It means to consider what you are reading. Meditating on the Word of God means thinking about what you have read and then applying it to your life.

Joshua was triumphant over his enemies. The Israelites, with God's help, conquered cities and established a nation based on His promise to them. If you are going to triumph over your spiritual enemies and establish yourself, you must base your life on God's Word. Daily devotion to the Word of God through reading and study is essential for living a life that unleashes heaven's blessings, a life in which there are no more limits.

> TO TRIUMPH OVER YOUR SPIRITUAL ENEMIES AND ESTABLISH YOURSELF, YOU MUST BASE YOUR LIFE ON GOD'S WORD.

DO NOT WORRY ABOUT DAILY NEEDS

Remember that Jesus not only taught His disciples to pray for their daily bread, but He also taught them not to worry about where it was going to come from.

> *Therefore do not worry, saying, "What shall we eat?" or "What shall we drink?" or "What shall we wear?"*   (Matthew 6:31)

When Jesus said, *"Do not worry,"* He did not mean that you are never to think about or pray about what you are going to eat or drink. He was saying that after you have prayed about your needs and trusted God for your daily bread, you are not to worry about your food, drink, or clothes; you are not to be anxious about how your needs will be fulfilled.

Anxious thoughts come to all of us at times, but some people seem to worry about everything. When you are worrying about your basic needs, you are failing to put God first in your life. You are demonstrating a lack of confidence and trust in His ability to answer your prayers and meet those needs.

Jesus went on to tell His disciples to establish their priorities in relation to God and His kingdom.

But seek first the kingdom of God and His righteousness, and all these things shall be added to you.   (Matthew 6:33)

When you make God your number one priority, you will never have to worry or be anxious about what you are going to eat, drink, or wear. God will provide these things for you when you pray.

Notice that when Jesus instructed us not to worry about what we would eat, drink, or wear, He was telling us not to talk negatively. If you have faith in God, you should already know the answer to these questions: God is going provide your food. God is going to provide your drink. God is going to provide your clothes. Do not worry or question how or by whom these things will come. Seek God first, and all these things will be provided for you in His perfect way.

RECEIVE PEACE FOR DAILY LIVING

Putting God first and trusting in Him to provide for your basic needs will enable you to live a peaceful life. The apostle Paul reinforced Jesus' admonition to pray and not worry when he wrote,

> *Be anxious for nothing, but in everything by prayer and supplication, with thanksgiving, let your requests be made known to God.*
> (Philippians 4:6)

Paul said not to worry but to pray. Pray about everything that is bothering you. Let all your needs be known to God. Then, after you ask Him to meet your needs, give thanks that He knows your needs. Give thanks that He hears your prayers. Thank Him for answering your prayers, and do not worry about them after you pray.

Are you seeking God in your life? Is He your top priority? If you are being obedient to Him and seeking Him, your needs will be met.

If you pray, "God, I don't want limitations in my life anymore," He will say, "That is good. You are on the right track. I will help you."

If you pray, "God, I don't want to lose my temper anymore," He will say, "I hear your prayer, and I will help you to develop the fruit of the Spirit in your life."

If you pray, "God, I am petitioning You for what I need, and I am thanking You right now that I am not going to be limited by fear anymore. I'm not going to worry, and I'm not going to be anxious for anything," God will say, "Keep it up. Keep petitioning Me for your needs, and keep thanking Me for the answers every day."

Paul said that after you have made your requests known to God and thanked Him for answering your prayers, *"the peace of God, which surpasses all understanding, will guard your hearts and minds through Christ Jesus"* (Philippians 4:7).

Once you pray with thanksgiving, there is a release. When you believe that God has heard your prayers and will answer them, the worries disappear, and peace floods your heart and mind.

> WHEN YOU BELIEVE THAT GOD HAS HEARD YOUR PRAYERS AND WILL ANSWER THEM, THE WORRIES DISAPPEAR.

The next verse in Philippians tells you how to *keep* peace in your heart and mind. After you have prayed, given thanks, and received peace, you must take control of your thoughts.

> *Finally, brethren, whatever things are true, whatever things are noble, whatever things are just, whatever things are pure, whatever things are lovely, whatever things are of good report, if there is any virtue and if there is anything praiseworthy; meditate on these things.* (verse 8)

Have you noticed that the things you worry about do not usually come to pass? Most of the time, the things that you spend time fretting about never happen.

Your mind might tell you the whole world is tumbling down around you. You might imagine obstacles and limitations that do not exist. Since most of these things will never occur in your life, why worry about them? Replace those negative thoughts with positive thoughts.

The Bible says to think about things that are good, just, honest, and pure. Stop filling your mind with negative thoughts, and you will enjoy the peace God gives your heart and mind after you pray.

DAILY HABITS YIELD RESULTS

The above are some important ways in which you can live one day at a time. Disciplined people develop good daily habits. You have to be disciplined at seeking God. When you become disciplined, you will start seeing results.

However, while you should read your Bible and pray daily, do not despair if you sometimes miss your prayer time and Bible reading, or if you make a mistake. I have pulled muscles when I've exercised. In time, I healed, and I did not quit exercising just because I had hurt myself. I simply stopped for a little while to mend, and then I started exercising again.

Similarly, if you make a mistake or fall down spiritually, ask God to forgive you so you can "mend." Say, "Father, I am sorry. I repent. Please forgive me." Do what you need to do to make it right. Forgive yourself. Forget it and move on with your life. Remember that renewing your mind and becoming conformed to the image of Jesus Christ is a process. A tree may not look like it is growing, but if it is healthy and receiving the proper nutrition and sunshine, it will grow. You are the same way. If you receive the proper spiritual nutrition and sunshine each day from praying and from reading the Bible and applying its truths to your life, you will grow. Daily spiritual growth will help you reach new levels of Christian maturity.

For example, suppose you pray, "Father, I am going to walk in Your divine favor today. I'm not going to become upset or be offended. I'm going to walk in Your perfect peace. I'm not going to be worried. Amen." After you pray this prayer, you go about your daily business when, suddenly, a situation arises that could cause you to become upset and worry. You may have missed the mark yesterday and the day before, but this time, something is different. You have been praying, and you have been reading your Bible daily. You have been keeping God first in your life. You have set a goal not to become angry and upset when circumstances seem to work against you. Now you realize you are not angry or upset at this situation. Yesterday, it would have bothered you, but today you have victory.

Whatever limitations you may be experiencing, if you continue to grow spiritually, you will find yourself conquering those limits. What used to bother you will no longer hold you back. Your limits will have been broken.

IF YOU CONTINUE TO GROW SPIRITUALLY, YOU WILL FIND YOURSELF CONQUERING WHATEVER LIMITATIONS YOU MAY BE EXPERIENCING.

Living a life that pleases God will remove hindrances from your life. Time will prove this true. Months from now, maybe even years from now, you will look back and see how you have changed. You will see how you have grown into a different person.

As you continue to grow on a daily basis, you will increase in many areas. Your giving to God's work will increase. Your energy will increase. Your prayer life will increase. Your spiritual vitality will increase. Your strength will increase. You will be amazed at the many ways in which you have broken through your limitations.

Living a triumphant daily life means you will keep expanding your boundaries. It means you will always glorify and please God, and your life will be filled with joy. This is the way life with Jesus was intended to be lived: abundantly and without limits, unleashing heaven's blessings.

EPILOGUE:
UNDERSTANDING
THE KINGDOM OF HEAVEN

A few years ago, I was invited to attend a seminar on Strategic Leadership for CEOs at the U.S. Army War College in Gettysburg, Pennsylvania. The first day of the seminar began with a strategic walk of the battlefield. The second day was spent in the war room learning and discussing strategy.

I learned that strategy is more than just how to get from point A to point B. Strategy is a system, an entire way of doing things. It is not just your immediate plan; it also includes what you ultimately hope to accomplish. In this way, a strategy becomes the system that produces the results you desire. Systems are utilized in a variety of organizations, from armies to corporations to ministries. The successes of their plans, goals, and products are the results of their systems.

HOW THE KINGDOM OF HEAVEN OPERATES

The kingdom of heaven also operates by various "strategies" and "systems," or ways of doing things. Applying the "systems" of the kingdom of heaven is the only way to unleash the potential of God in your life, receive His blessings, and overcome all limitations. This is what Jesus was explaining to Peter when He said, *"And I will give you the keys of the kingdom of heaven, and whatever you bind on earth will be bound in heaven, and whatever you loose on earth will be loosed in heaven"* (Matthew 16:19). Jesus told His disciples to pray, *"Your will be done on earth as it is in heaven"* (Matthew 6:10). In other words, the ways God thinks and acts in heaven are the ways we are to think and act on earth. Literally, the kingdom of heaven means "the kingdom from the heavens." The sovereignty is from heaven because the King is there. (See John 18:36.) We will never totally unleash our potential in God until we understand this revelation.

THE WAYS GOD THINKS AND ACTS IN HEAVEN ARE THE WAYS WE ARE TO THINK AND ACT ON EARTH.

We also need to realize that our authority to implement the heavenly system comes from our relationship to Christ and the fact that we reign with Him. The apostle Paul understood his identity in Christ, and he wrote, *"I have been crucified with Christ; it is no longer I who live, but Christ lives in me; and the life which I now live in the flesh I live by faith in the Son of God"* (Galatians 2:20). Furthermore, he said, *"If then you were raised with Christ, seek those things which are above, where Christ is, sitting at the right hand of God. Set your mind [including your understanding] on things above, not on things on the earth"* (Colossians 3:1–2).

Paul was instructing us to focus on the "system" by which heaven operates. To further illustrate this principle, let's refer to Moses' construction of the earthly tabernacle.

> [Israel's priests] *serve the copy and shadow of the heavenly things, as Moses was divinely instructed when he was about to make the tabernacle. For He said, "See that you make all things according to the pattern shown you on the mountain."*
>
> (Hebrews 8:5)

In Paul's teachings, he was not telling us just to think about how wonderful it will be when we get to heaven. Heaven is wonderful, but we are not there yet; we are here. We are a heavenly people living on earth to demonstrate a heavenly system.

THE CALLING OF THE CHURCH

Jesus said, *"All authority has been given to Me in heaven and on earth. Go therefore..."* (Matthew 28:18–19). He plainly delegated His power (*"in heaven and on earth"*) to the church. (See Matthew 16:19.) The church's calling, or mission, can therefore be summarized in these four statements:

1. To bring people to the knowledge of the truth. (See John 8:31–32; 1 Timothy 2:1–4; Ephesians 4:11–15.)

2. To open people's eyes and turn them from darkness to light. (See Acts 26:14–18; Colossians 1:12–14.)

3. To shine as lights and preserve as salt. (See Matthew 5:13–16; Philippians 2:15.)

4. To prepare for eternal service as rulers over earthly nations. (See Luke 19:17–19; Revelation 2:26–28.)

The only possible way to accomplish these tasks is to understand and apply the strategies of the kingdom of heaven.

UNLEASHING GOD'S PROMISES

As we set our minds on heavenly things, the Holy Spirit will reveal God's systems and strategies to us. Remember, systems are not altogether foreign to us. The laws of prosperity, seedtime and harvest, and sowing and reaping are all systems and strategies used in the kingdom of heaven. (For example, read and study the explanation of the parable of the sower in Mark 4:14–32.) The laws that govern healing and deliverance are clearly given to us by Jesus Himself. (See, for example, Mark 16:17–18.) The laws that govern salvation are also revealed for those who believe. (See, for example, Romans 10:9–10.)

These heavenly systems are not hidden from us. God has revealed them to us through Jesus.

> *His divine power has given to us all things that pertain to life and godliness, through the knowledge of Him who called us by glory and virtue, by which have been given to us exceedingly great and precious promises, that through these you may be* **partakers of the divine nature.***"*
>
> (2 Peter 1:3–4, emphasis added)

Even though *"all things that pertain to life and godliness"* might be invisible to us at present, God has given us the force of faith to unleash them in our lives. Jesus made a profound statement concerning the kingdom of heaven: *"The kingdom of heaven has been forcefully advancing, and forceful men lay hold of it"* (Matthew 11:12 NIV).

Faith (acting on what you know) is the substance of things hoped for. (See Hebrews 11:1.) Faith will manifest heavenly things on earth. In Mark 11:22, where Jesus said, *"Have faith in God,"* the phrase literally means "Have the faith of God." Faith is the *currency* of the kingdom of heaven; it's how we unleash our godly potential and overcome all limitations in our lives.

> FAITH IS THE CURRENCY OF THE KINGDOM OF HEAVEN; IT'S HOW WE UNLEASH OUR GODLY POTENTIAL AND OVERCOME ALL LIMITATIONS IN OUR LIVES.

We have seen that faith is released through the words we speak. Faith calls for those heavenly things that do not yet exist on earth to be as though they did exist here...because they are a reality; they are already accomplished in the Spirit. (See Romans 4:17.) You don't perceive them yet with your natural senses, but they exist in the kingdom of heaven. (See 2 Corinthians 4:18.) I realize this concept may be spiritually deep for some Christians. Yet the purpose of this book is to show you how to unleash your God-given potential and overcome your limitations, including the limits of your understanding.

God's Word is *"incorruptible"* (1 Peter 1:23) and produces faith. (See Romans 10:17.) It will achieve that which pleases Him, and it will not return to Him void. (See Isaiah 55:10–11.) His Word is like seed, and we will reap what we sow. (See Galatians 6:7.) Confessing the promises of heavenly things is sowing the seed of faith for what you need. It's the way the kingdom of heaven works. And it's the way we unleash heaven's blessings into our earthly lives.

About the Author

In 1979, God spoke to Happy Caldwell to build a spiritual production center in Little Rock, Arkansas, in order to take the good news of Jesus Christ to the city, state, nation, and world. Happy and his wife, Jeanne, founded Agape Church, a strong, Spirit-filled body of believers. Through Happy's deep sensitivity to the Spirit of God and his anointed teaching, the lost are being saved, the sick are being healed, and thousands are being blessed.

Also desiring to see spiritual excellence in education, Agape expanded its ministry to include Agape Academy and Agape College, which offers both diploma and degree programs.

In 1988, Happy and Jeanne answered a direct call from the Lord to take His message beyond central Arkansas. They founded VTN—the Victory Television Network. This network of three full-power TV stations is carried on more than 200 cable systems and is bringing the gospel into more than 1.2 million households. Through his own daily program, *Arkansas Alive*, Happy presents the Word in profound simplicity, making the character of God a revelation to those who hear. He has also recorded several musical albums with Jeanne.

Happy's ministry is known for instilling Christian principles in strategic leadership. He was honored for this in 2005 with an invitation to participate in the U.S. Army War College Strategic Leader Staff Ride at Gettysburg, Pennsylvania.

He is a recipient of the Peter J. Daniels Caleb Encourager Award, which has been bestowed upon such notable people as Norman Vincent Peale, Nelson Mandela, and Dr. Oral Roberts. He has also been recognized by the Arkansas Martin Luther King Jr. Commission with The Salute to Greatness Community Service Award.

Happy Caldwell has written several other books, including *Saving Our Cities*, *An Expected End*, and *How to Thrive in Perilous Times*. He continues to travel worldwide, delivering the life-changing message of Jesus Christ.